30 STRATEGIES TO BUILD LITERACY SKILLS

Bringing the
COMMON
CORE *to* LIFE

in K–8 Classrooms

ERIC JENSEN

LEANN NICKELSEN

Solution Tree | Press

a division of
Solution Tree

555 North Morton Street
Bloomington, IN 47404
800.733.6786 (toll free) / 812.336.7700
FAX: 812.336.7790
email: info@solution-tree.com
solution-tree.com

Visit **go.solution-tree.com/commoncore** to download reproducibles and access live links from this book.

Printed in the United States of America

17 16 15 14   3 4 5

Library of Congress Cataloging-in-Publication Data
Jensen, Eric, 1950 author.
   Bringing the common core to life in K-8 classrooms : 30 strategies to build literacy skills / Eric Jensen, LeAnn Nickelsen.
      pages cm
   Includes bibliographical references and index.
   ISBN 978-1-936764-64-8 (perfect bound) 1. Language arts (Elementary)--Curricula--United States. 2. Language arts (Middle School)--Curricula--United States. 3. Language arts (Elementary)--Standards--United States. 4. Language arts (Middle School)--Standards--United States. I. Title.
   LB1576.J44 2014
   372.6--dc23   2013037573

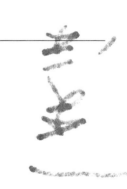

Solution Tree
Jeffrey C. Jones, CEO
Edmund M. Ackerman, President

Solution Tree Press
President: Douglas M. Rife
Editorial Director: Lesley Bolton
Managing Production Editor: Caroline Weiss
Production Editor: Rachel Rosolina
Proofreader: Elisabeth Abrams
Cover Designer: Rian Anderson
Text Designer: Laura Kagemann

This is dedicated to all the teachers who are passionate, lifelong learners. Your thirst for learning is what helps kids succeed as much as all of the skills and compassion you bring every day. Thank you. —Eric

I dedicate this book . . .

to Leslie Goodwin, my good friend, who went to her eternal home after battling a brain tumor. Thank you for teaching me so much about our most important purpose in life. You are greatly missed. (Sadie and Connor, your mom was the best teacher—she taught by example!)

to my husband of twenty-two years, Joel. I'm so grateful for your support, love, and friendship. Thank you for always encouraging my educational passions and efforts.

to my twin children, Keaton and Aubrey, who are in high school. May your learning journey give you joy, passion, and a mission to help others and yourselves become the best you can be. Thank you for helping me understand the learning process so much better through your educational experiences.

to all the educators who have touched my life and helped me become a better teacher and person (to name a few: my mom, Dolores Heim, who is a retired teacher, and Laura Smith and Sharon McClelland, who taught me how to teach). —LeAnn

ACKNOWLEDGMENTS

Thank you to:

Our editors Douglas Rife, for his faith in the project, and Rachel Rosolina, for endless commitment to the quality of the manuscript (you have been amazing!). Thank you to Lesley Bolton for always checking in and helping with this process.

Melissa Dickson, friend and fellow educational consultant, for contributing to the instructional Cha-Cha-Chas song, for contributing to our learning, and for being one of the strongest people I know!

Dr. Katie McKnight, friend and fellow educational consultant, for proofing the first draft and giving us great feedback to improve the book.

Anne Arundel County, Maryland, teachers, special education department, and principals—you have been amazing to work with the past three years and have taught me so much. Thank you for implementing many of these strategies into your classrooms. Those students are so blessed to have you! Martha Lehman, Bobbi Pedrick, Pam Courson, and Marty McCleaf—you have been amazing to work with for three years!

Linda Allen, friend, colleague, and coauthor with LeAnn on *Making Words Their Own*, for her ideas within the strategy List-Sort-Label-Write.

Melissa Dickson, Anne Arundel County educators, and Rowan-Salisbury, North Carolina, educators for their contributions to the Cruisin' Clipboard form.

Anna Ory, MacArthur Middle School teacher in Anne Arundel County Schools, for great ideas for making Interactive Notebooks more organized.

Science teachers at Scotts Ridge Middle School in Ridgefield, Connecticut, for sample Interactive Notebooks.

North Carolina's Rowan-Salisbury Schools teachers, curriculum coordinators, assistant superintendent, AIG and EL coordinators, and principals. Your quick hunger for and implementation of many of these strategies were amazing to me. Thank you for your feedback about the strategies and for making them better. Those students are so blessed to have you!

Eric Jensen—thank you for the opportunity to write with you once again. I learn so much from you!

—LeAnn

Solution Tree Press would like to thank the following reviewers:

Amy Benjamin
Education Consultant
Amy Benjamin Educational Services
Fishkill, New York

Leslie S. Cook
Associate Professor, Department of Education
Appalachian State University
Boone, North Carolina

Shan Glandon
Director of Curriculum
Jenks Public Schools
Jenks, Oklahoma

Paul Goldberg
Principal
John Muir Literacy Academy
Hoffman Estates, Illinois

Katherine McKnight
Professor of Secondary Education
National Louis University
Chicago, Illinois

Tonika Peavy
Principal
South Plaquemines Elementary School
Port Sulphur, Louisiana

Visit **go.solution-tree.com/commoncore** to download
reproducibles and access live links from this book.

TABLE OF CONTENTS

Reproducible pages are in italics.

ABOUT THE AUTHORS

Eric Jensen is a former teacher who has taught students from the elementary level through the university level. Jensen cofounded SuperCamp, the United States' most innovative and largest academic enrichment program, now with nearly sixty thousand graduates. He has authored twenty-nine books, including *Engaging Students With Poverty in Mind*, *Enriching the Brain*, *Student Success Secrets*, *Teaching With the Brain in Mind*, *Super Teaching*, and *Teaching With Poverty in Mind*.

Jensen's academic background includes a bachelor of arts in English and a master of arts in organizational development, and he is now completing his doctorate. Jensen has made over fifty-five visits to neuroscience labs and interacts with countless neuroscientists. He is deeply committed to making a positive, significant, lasting difference in the way we learn. Currently, Jensen does staff development, conference speaking, and in-depth trainings. To learn more about Jensen's public programs, visit www.jensenlearning.com or follow @EricJensenBrain on Twitter.

LeAnn Nickelsen, EdM, educator for over twenty years, delivers presentations in the United States and internationally on brain research topics, differentiation, literacy strategies, Common Core State Standards, and engagement strategies. She was a classroom teacher in three states and won a Teacher of the Year award in Texas. Nickelsen is known as "the teacher's teacher" because of her practical, research-based examples that teachers can easily implement in their classrooms. She has a passion for instilling a love for learning in teachers and their students and helping learners reach their educational goals daily.

This is the second book she's coauthored with Eric Jensen; *Deeper Learning* was the first. She has also coauthored books on vocabulary and differentiation. She is the author of eight books, including *Memorizing Strategies & Other Brain-Based Activities* and the four-series set *Comprehension Mini-Lessons*. To learn more about Nickelsen's work, visit www.maximizelearninginc.com or follow @lnickelsen1 on Twitter.

To book Eric Jensen or LeAnn Nickelsen for professional development, contact pd@solution-tree.com.

INTRODUCTION

The term *engagement* is front and center for most educators. Our jobs allow us the opportunity to visit classrooms across the United States, and we have found we can categorize most classrooms into two broad categories based on their level of student engagement: top-down, passive classrooms and two-way, engaged-for-success classrooms.

When walking into a top-down, passive classroom, we see students in rows of chairs trying to stay awake or occupying their minds in other ways. Behavior extremes are rampant—from sleeping and daydreaming to emotional outbursts or disrespect. We witness little explicit instruction from the teacher guiding students to the learning goal or from student self-assessment; rather, we see a lot of "learn it yourself" worksheets and "do it my way or else" instruction. Students use outdated textbooks that are way above or below their reading levels and are labeled by the kids as uninteresting. Teachers give insufficient or vague feedback and do little to move the students along on the learning continuum.

The teacher controls most of the learning here; she tells students when to think and how to think, resulting in little exploration or thinking outside the box. Summative assessments do not match what is taught, causing discouragement and learned helplessness among many learners. Cognitive engagement might last for a few minutes as students seek to understand what is required to complete a worksheet, but most of the time, the brain suffers from "boring-itis." There is little joy in this classroom.

When entering a two-way, engaged-for-success classroom, the teacher invites us in with a smile and a nod. Here, we can see how much the students own their learning and their classroom. They are highly motivated because of the challenging, higher-level thinking opportunities they are given. They are enthused at being slightly out of their comfort zone, and they experience their learning in a variety of manners—even with other students. The teacher guides them through relevant, rigorous standards; facilitates engaging activities to get them there; and encourages them to create their own questions about what they're learning. There are very few behavioral problems because students are held accountable for thinking throughout the lesson. They take time to explore their questions through a variety of highly engaging strategies and activities. Students' memory of concepts is amazing—twenty-four hours and beyond. This teacher constantly gives students feedback, encouraging them to do better in relation to their readiness levels and standards. Students self-evaluate and give other students feedback as well. These students go home exhausted because they did so much thinking yet are exhilarated because of what they learned. In fact, they love learning and look forward to coming back tomorrow.

Every school has teaching stars who consistently outperform the others. What do those classrooms look and sound like? Probably very similar to the two-way classroom, as this type of classroom purposefully engages all students. If we want our students to enjoy and participate in the learning process, remember what was learned, apply the information at higher levels, and feel the content is valued and respected, then we must engage them. Engaging classrooms become a reality when teachers plan for them!

The Common Core State Standards

The Common Core State Standards (CCSS) require higher-level engagement among all students. The authors of the CCSS divide the English language arts (ELA) grade-level standards into grades K–5 and 6–12 (see figure 1.1). The division shows the emphasis on literacy skills in all classrooms—not just the ELA classrooms. There are four strands for grades K–5 and 6–12 ELA: Reading, Writing, Speaking and Listening, and Language. There are two strands for grades 6–12 literacy: Reading and Writing. These strands are then broken down into grade-level standards. For instance, in grades K–5, the Reading strand divides into separate standards for literature, informational text, and foundational skills. In addition, the Reading strand for grades 6–12 literacy incorporates the interdisciplinary standards of history / social studies and science and technical subjects.

One of the main goals of the CCSS is to make students proficient readers of complex texts in a variety of content areas. Extensive research from *Reading Between the Lines: What the ACT Reveals About College Readiness in Reading* (ACT, 2006) shows the need for college- and career-ready students to comprehend these types of challenging, informational texts. To achieve this level of comprehension, the authors of the CCSS created overarching college and career readiness anchor standards to clarify the intended learning progression from one grade level to the next.

In this text, we will focus on these anchor standards as guideposts. Throughout, we will reference these standards using the CCSS dot notation system. Each begins with "CCRA" to denote it is a college and career readiness anchor standard rather than a grade-level standard. Next comes the strand initial (R = Reading, W = Writing, SL = Speaking and Listening, or L = Language), which is followed by the anchor standard number. For instance, anchor standard two in the Writing strand would appear as: CCRA.W.2. (Visit www .corestandards.org/ELA-Literacy to see all ELA anchor standards and grade-level standards.)

While the CCSS define *what* all students are expected to know and be able to do, they do not dictate *how* to get them there. This book offers you some of the *hows* for literacy instruction across the content areas. Each of the thirty powerful engagement strategies in this book explains which CCSS components it includes so you understand how to get students from the standard to the learning goal while staying sane. These engagement strategies can be used in any classroom with any content, including language arts, social studies, science, and even some mathematics classrooms. We'll also show you how to structure instruction so that teaching becomes smarter rather than harder, ensuring that educators and administrators understand the best thinking tools to help all students achieve success with the CCSS. Finally, we'll help you remove the stress, concerns, and fear from your planning and instruction time and replace them with student enjoyment of the learning process.

The Three Engagement Zones

In order to make the levels of engagement easy to understand, we've categorized all strategies into three engagement zones. Each zone builds on the previous. The goal is to use at least one zone per lesson to ensure engagement.

Zone 1: Engage to Build Basics includes strategies for building background knowledge and activating prior knowledge. It covers foundational strategies that prepare the brain for more learning. Zone 2: Engage to Explore builds on Zone 1; it includes strategies for researching content more deeply. The CCSS ask students to engage in the research process in a quick and efficient manner, and this zone will guide all students in accomplishing this task. Zone 3: Engage to Own goes a step further; it includes strategies to help students invest in the content. Some of the strategies will help students engage in close reading strategies; they can't help but develop, synthesize, and own that content. Learning becomes extremely deep when close reading occurs. Other strategies in Zone 3 will help all content area teachers guide their students successfully through the close reading of complex texts. We want students to own their content by engaging emotionally with the content, forming opinions, and arguing for a perspective they believe strongly in.

See chapter 3 for more information about the three engagement zones.

Overview of Chapters

Chapters 1–3 offer an introductory look at engagement in relation to the CCSS. In chapter 1, you will discover exactly what an engaged classroom looks and sounds like. We will share a list of the criteria for engagement so that we can relate every strategy to how it engages students. In chapter 2, we further explain the CCSS ELA strands—especially Reading and Writing, which will be the focus of this book. By chapter 3, we're ready to tie the CCSS and our three engagement zones together with step-by-step instructions for designing a daily target.

Chapters 4 and 5 discuss Zone 1: Engage to Build Basics and are great for the beginning of a unit. Chapter 4 delves deeper into the goals of Zone 1, exploring the science behind jumpstarting the brain and providing ideas of when to use Zone 1 as well as verbs to use when building a powerful Zone 1 target. Even students who have extremely limited background

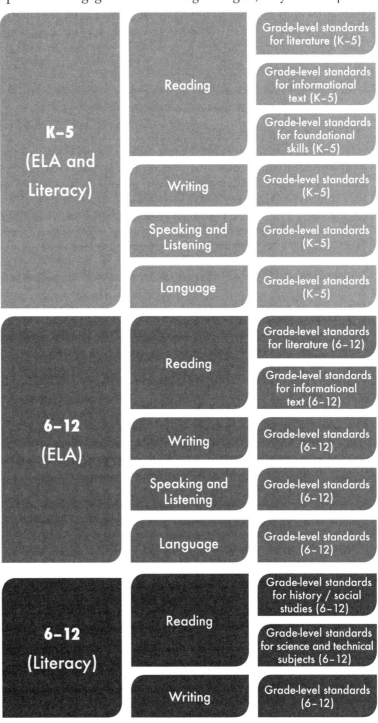

Figure I.1: Organization of the CCSS ELA.

Source: Adapted from Marzano, Yanoski, Hoegh, & Simms (2013), p. 13.

knowledge can be successful with strategies from this zone. In chapter 5, you'll discover ten Zone 1 strategies that focus on building background knowledge and activating students' prior knowledge. Each strategy in this book includes sections on preparation and materials, instructions, and assessment in order for you to easily incorporate it into your classroom.

By chapter 6, you're ready to bump it up a notch with Zone 2: Engage to Explore. Here, you'll learn how questions can keep students engaged. We also provide ideas of when to use Zone 2 and a list of verbs to use when building a powerful Zone 2 target. In chapter 7, you'll find nine Zone 2 strategies for incorporating research into your classroom.

By chapter 8, we're ready for the grand finale—Zone 3: Engage to Own. The standards requiring the close reading of complex texts are the focus of this chapter. Here, we will explore the concept of close reading and provide ideas of when to use Zone 3 and a list of verbs to use when building a powerful Zone 3 target. In chapter 9, we give you eleven Zone 3 strategies that promote passion and ownership of content.

Finally, chapter 10 helps you plan the big picture: the unit. Once you have a unit planned, we'll show you how to break that down into lesson plans created from specific targets. Then we cover the role of formative assessment and how to work in differentiated changes throughout your unit to ensure you reach all students. This chapter ends with advice on creating transformative habits, finding the support necessary to use these strategies, and learning the role of self-empowerment. We want you to habitually engage your students, create new teaching habits, and replace ineffective habits.

Each chapter ends with ASQ Time, which is an opportunity to decide on an action step, summarize your learning, and come up with questions; this is your chance to reflect on the chapter and record next steps.

Last but not least, appendix A provides you an entire list of ways to differentiate any strategy in this book, and appendix B connects each of the thirty engagement strategies to applicable anchor standards.

With this preview of coming attractions, we hope you're excited. This book has the capacity to transform your teaching and, in doing so, raise the academic achievement of your students. You'll be up to speed in two vital areas. The CCSS are, of course, critical, and you'll be able to refer to them with confidence. The engagement strategies will make your teaching more fun and help your students succeed every single day. We're glad you have chosen this resource. Get ready to rock on!

CHAPTER 1

SUCCESS FORMULA FOR ENGAGEMENT

Give kids a chance to talk, and they'll tell you what engagement is to them. An Indiana University survey asked eighty-one thousand high school students to name their favorite learning strategies at school. The survey, titled "Charting the Path From Engagement to Achievement," provides an in-depth look at student preferences (Yazzie-Mintz, 2010). Sixty-six percent of these students said they are bored, and 82 percent want more opportunities to be creative. Many of them prefer discussing and debating what they learned (61 percent). They want to engage in group projects (60 percent) and have the option to use technology for projects and lessons (55 percent). Nearly half (46 percent) enjoy presenting what they learned. Other popular strategies include role-playing (43 percent) and using art and drama to express what they learned (49 percent). Only 6 percent of the students said they liked lecture. In other words, they are screaming out loud, "Let us actually DO SOMETHING!"

Students want to get involved! They want to be engaged with what they're learning and with other students to make the content more meaningful and relevant. This is far preferred to sitting in a chair and regurgitating simple learning that was acquired through teacher lectures or a worksheet.

In this chapter, we focus on understanding engaged learning and fostering an engaging climate.

Understanding Engaged Learning

So often we think that if students are busy, they are engaged and, therefore, learning. Engaging students involves much more than simply keeping them busy. Being cognitively engaged often refers to a student willingly investing sustained, focused attention and effort toward a cognitively challenging learning task (the task could be mental, emotional, spiritual, or physical). Being fully engaged means the student is self-regulating the learning and managing the steps necessary to accomplish a goal. Having autonomy and personal control over the process is associated with a high form of cognitive engagement and motivation.

According to Helen Marks (2000), engagement is a "psychological process, specifically, the attention, interest, and investment and effort students expend in the work of learning" (pp. 154–155). There are at least three types of classroom-based engagement: (1) affective, (2) behavioral, and (3) cognitive (Fredericks, Blumenfeld, & Paris, 2004). *Affective engagement* is all about the emotions and emotional reactions of the learner during the learning process—the greater the student's interest level, positive affect, positive attitude, curiosity, and task absorption, the greater the affective engagement. *Behavioral engagement* is all about student on-task behavior. The student's effort and persistence in combination with his or her level of attention (and ability to divert attention away from distractions), related questions, and ability to seek help enable the student to accomplish the task at hand. *Cognitive engagement*—which is the heart of this text—ranges from simple, easier work (such as call-and-response) to highly complex problem solving in a social context. While we will describe some simple engagement strategies, our focus will be on more complex engagement strategies, since that is the destination of the Common Core State Standards.

Engagement can also be defined by its length, social conditions, amount of physical movement, and involvement of emotions. For instance, some of the strategies in this book are engaging because students are placed into small groups, while others demand kinesthetic tactics. All of the strategies evoke some type of positive learning emotion.

The CCSS have an overarching goal of more student independence and more self-regulation of learning. So why not give students the exact list of engagement criteria and ask them to rate themselves? Ultimately, the best person to determine whether a lesson was engaging is the student. To this end, we created quick-rating checklist reproducibles that cover possible criteria for engagement (see pages 9–11 or visit **go.solution-tree.com/commoncore** to download). We offer a checklist for younger students and a second checklist, which is more advanced and open ended, for older students. Have students fill out this form periodically to determine whether or not they are engaged at high levels, and use it as a guide for adjusting your instruction. Students need to be in charge of regulating their engagement, but as teachers, we need to create an environment where engagement can occur.

Fostering an Engaging Climate

Our environments greatly affect how well we stay engaged in learning. For example, when we are tired, hungry, thirsty, stressed, uncomfortable, or feeling unsafe or unloved, our brains most likely will not stay as engaged for long periods. We also know that just the right amount of stress enhances learning and memory (Vedhara, Hyde, Gilchrist, Tytherleigh, & Plummer, 2000). Challenge in a supportive environment is the impetus for cognitive engagement.

The classroom's climate is highly dependent on the teacher's attitude. While your level of effectiveness when instructing your students is extremely important, engagement starts with your overall mood and attitudes. You'll engage more students with honey than with vinegar. Your presence affects your relationship with the student, and your positive body language and attitude will help make every single strategy in this book work easier and better. Two key ingredients for a positive relationship with your students are (1) connecting with your students to show you are interested in their lives and (2) differentiating instruction by responding to individual students' needs.

Connecting With Your Students

There are several ways to connect with your students daily: give high fives when they enter or leave the classroom, write notes of encouragement, give positive feedback to help them grow in their understanding of the daily target, smile and gesture during lessons, invite them for lunch in the classroom, celebrate achievements, ask questions about their lives outside school, care about their trials, and gear lessons toward their interests. The latter idea tends to be the most challenging to implement when there is such a broad curriculum. Yet, the more interested we are in the topic, the easier it is to excel.

Connect with their interests using a "Who Are You?" Interest Inventory (Jensen & Nickelsen, 2008; see page 12 for a reproducible or visit **go.solution-tree.com/commoncore** to download). Ask what they do in their spare time, what sports they like to play and watch, what genre of books they read, and overall, what they enjoy. For younger students, you can read the inventory aloud and have them answer the questions verbally. The answers will help you understand that student better and enable you to reach out to him or her in a way that will encourage a love for learning.

A *learning profile* can help you organize all of this valuable information. Just create a file folder for each student with relevant information, like the interest inventory. We use learning profiles ourselves, and anytime we need to understand a student better, create choices, reteach, help a student become an expert, or group students, we look at that student's learning profile to assist us (Jensen & Nickelsen, 2008). We also want students to know how they learn best, and these inventories will help them better understand themselves as learners. Students are welcome to keep the folder up to date, and we recommend revisiting the pieces in January since students change so much throughout the school year. Other information to include in a learning profile might be:

- **Strengths**—Parents will commonly talk about their own children as being very tech-savvy, musical, street smart, or hands on. These descriptions are typical of the varieties of ways that kids show their strengths.

- **Emotional intelligence**—Evidence suggests that social-emotional skills contribute to academic achievement (Durlak, Weissberg, Dymnicki, Taylor, & Schellingar, 2011). This is why it's important to value not only the skills of accurately perceiving emotions in self and others, using emotions to facilitate thinking, understanding emotions, and managing emotions but also programs or processes that build these skills.

- **Learning preferences**—We all have preferences when it comes to learning comfortably. For example, some prefer to work in small groups while others would rather learn independently. Some prefer to hear classical music during writing while others prefer no noise at all. For learning preference questions and questions about subject area interests and strengths, see pages 13–16 for reproducibles or visit **go.solution-tree.com/commoncore** to download.

- **Observations**—Notes from previous teachers about a student's subject or test experiences can give current teachers great insight into the student's background knowledge as well as behavior and preferences.

Not only will connecting with your students improve your classroom climate, but it will also set an example for how students interact with one another daily. Setting high expectations for cooperative learning during group work is vital. Pointing out and praising good social interactions is key to improving social skills all day long.

Differentiating Instruction

This second ingredient is foundational for a positive learning climate and daily success with each student. Differentiation is about using various strategies, materials, and tools to help all students reach the standards they need for success. It involves changing the content, thinking processes, pace of instruction, or assessments so each student can get to the standard. Teachers need a powerful growth mindset to help all students reach the standard or daily outcome, knowing students will arrive via different strategies on different days. Differentiation is meeting a student's learning needs individually or in a small group so he or she can attain the learning target. Rick Wormeli (2006), speaking on differentiation and assessment, often says what is fair isn't always equal. Differentiation is giving students what they need when they need it so they can be successful. In addition, we must teach students powerful, engaging, research-based strategies that they can pull from their toolbox to self-regulate their learning and attain their goals.

Giving students choices encourages them to learn more about their interests and empowers them to choose strategies that help them learn. Appropriate choice encourages autonomy building, which in turn contributes to greater engagement and achievement (Hafen et al., 2012). At the elementary level, autonomy also helps develop greater independence, which can foster motivation (Zee, Koomen, & Van der Veen, 2013).

When giving choices, however, be careful to ensure that all choices set your students up for success with your standards. Every assignment, question, activity, and strategy that we use within our lessons must help our students get to the daily target.

Chapter 10 (page 183) explores differentiation across a unit, and appendix A (page 197) has a list of ways to differentiate the strategies in this book. It's important to choose what's right for your students, and we'll show you how to modify strategies to suit the specific needs of your students. After all, there is no "one size fits all" engagement strategy.

Conclusion

Now that engagement has been defined and characterized, you will see how the strategies in this book energize brains to master the standards as well as your daily targets. When we know our students, know effective teaching practices such as differentiation, know how to engage, and have a positive, growth mindset, we are ready to use strategies that help our students grasp the Common Core State Standards faster and in more enjoyable ways. In the next chapter, we'll explore the demands of these standards.

ASQ Time

1. **Action step:** What is the single most valuable next step you will take after having read this chapter?

2. **Summary of learning:** Summarize in three to five sentences what you learned in this chapter.

3. **Question:** What discussion questions do you have for other readers, for the authors, or for self-reflection to explore more from this chapter?

Criteria for Engagement: Primary (Grades K–3)

CRITERIA	RATE YOURSELF Rate your engagement level for each criterion by marking the continuum with an X.		EXPLAIN
Eagerness to Learn	1 = I was not interested in learning this lesson. It seemed boring and unimportant, and it was not relevant to me.	4 = I was eager to learn this information or skill. It seemed interesting, important, and relevant to me. I was sure I could do this.	
Ability to Learn	1 = I was unclear what we were supposed to do, and I was also unsure if I knew how to do it. I didn't have a good attitude.	4 = I knew what we were supposed to do. I knew I had what it takes and how to do it. I positively approached the learning opportunities.	
Level of Preparedness	1 = I didn't have any of my supplies. I was a bit scattered and didn't get much done today.	4 = I had the supplies ready to go. My mind stayed focused. When finished, I knew what else to do.	
Eagerness to Participate	1 = I didn't respond or contribute today. I was off task and didn't feel like being a part of the learning.	4 = I responded in my small groups and in the whole-group discussion with statements that showed I was learning.	
Ability to Master Content	1 = I was very confused. I have no idea what was going on today. I struggled a lot!	4 = I showed evidence of learning the target. I struggled a little but kept going!	

Total Points: _____

Criteria for Engagement: Intermediate (Grades 4–8)

CRITERIA	RATE 2 = YES! 1 = SORT OF 0 = NO!	EXPLAIN
Eagerness to Learn		
The content was relevant to my life now and in the future.		
The content was focused on my interests.		
The content seemed important to learn; the purpose for learning was set.		
There was a sense of fun and joy during the learning that kept me on task.		
Ability to Learn		
I understood the learning targets.		
I could list the criteria to get there.		
I had a good attitude while learning today.		
Level of Preparedness		
The activities and content grabbed my attention.		
I used self-regulation strategies to stay focused on tasks.		
I had the supplies needed to successfully work.		
I used my time wisely.		

CRITERIA	RATE 2 = YES! 1 = SORT OF 0 = NO!	EXPLAIN
Eagerness to Participate		
I put forth effort to achieve the target.		
I asked and answered questions.		
I worked with other students; we gave each other feedback and helped one another get to the target.		
Ability to Master Content		
I struggled a little but persisted until I met the goal.		
I did a lot of thinking to accomplish the task.		

Questions I have about today's learning:

"Who Are You?" Interest Inventory

Name: _____

Date: _____

1. What are your favorite hobbies?

2. What are your favorite books AND types (genres) of books to read?

3. What are your favorite games to play (board games, card games, and so on)?

4. What are your favorite sports that you play? What sports do you like to watch?

5. If you had two hours to do whatever you wanted, what would you do?

6. What are your favorite subjects in school, and why?

7. What are your not-so-favorite subjects in school, and why?

8. What career interests you the most?

9. If you went to the library and had to check out nonfiction books, what topics would you choose?

10. What would you like me to know about you (strengths, growth opportunities, and so on)?

11. What clubs or committees are you currently on? Last year? Future ones you plan to be on?

12. Is there something that nobody in this class knows about you? Something unique about yourself? This will be kept secret if you want it to.

Jensen, E., & Nickelsen, L. (2008). Deeper learning: 7 powerful strategies for in-depth and longer-lasting learning. *Thousand Oaks, CA: Corwin Press.*

Learning Preferences: Primary (Grades K-3)

Name: _____

Date: _____

Directions: Circle your favorite between the two choices. *(Note: For nonreaders, just do this interview style.)*

I would like to learn . . .

1. By myself OR in a small group

2. While listening to music OR while there is little noise in the room

3. By drawing a picture OR writing

4. By solving story problems OR adding or subtracting lists of numbers

5. Near a window OR away from a window

6. In the front of the room OR in the back of the room

7. At my desk OR on the carpet on the floor

8. By typing my words OR by writing my words

9. By being the leader of a group OR by being a part of a group

10. In the morning OR in the afternoon

Jensen, E., & Nickelsen, L. (2008). Deeper learning: 7 powerful strategies for in-depth and longer-lasting learning. *Thousand Oaks, CA: Corwin Press.*

Learning Preferences: Intermediate (Grades 4–8)

Name: _____

Date: _____

Directions: Circle one of the following and then explain why you circled it. Would you rather:

1. Learn in a small group OR independently?

    Why: _____

2. Listen to music while learning OR have very little noise in the classroom?

    Why: _____

3. Learn new, complex information in the morning OR afternoon?

    Why: _____

4. Draw a concept OR write about it OR web it?

    Why: _____

5. Do math computations (equation solving) OR solve math word problems?

    Why: _____

6. Sit next to a window OR sit up front OR sit in the back OR sit in the middle of the classroom?

    Why: _____

7. Gather information by reading a book OR searching the Internet OR interviewing somebody OR taking notes from the teacher?

    Why: _____

8. Write information OR type information OR speak the information?

    Why: _____

9. Be a leader of a group OR a participant of a group?

    Why: _____

10. Work with a partner OR work with a small group of about three to four students?

    Why: _____

Jensen, E., & Nickelsen, L. (2008). Deeper learning: 7 powerful strategies for in-depth and longer-lasting learning. *Thousand Oaks, CA: Corwin Press.*

Subject Area Interests and Strengths: Primary (Grades K–3)

Directions: Rate the following school subjects based on your interest and your strength with a smiley face, neutral face, or unhappy face.

Interest:

(I like this topic. I'm curious about this subject. I would like to explore this topic in more depth in my spare time.)

☹ = I just do not have much interest in this subject.

😐 = I am sometimes interested in this subject.

☺ = I am very interested in this subject.

Strength:

☹ = I am not very good at this subject.

😐 = I am somewhat good at this subject.

☺ = I am very good at this subject.

SUBJECT	INTEREST	STRENGTH
Math		
Science		
Social Studies		
Reading		
Writing		
Spelling		
P.E.		
Music		
Art		
Computer Class		
Foreign Language		

Jensen, E., & Nickelsen, L. (2008). Deeper learning: 7 powerful strategies for in-depth and longer-lasting learning. *Thousand Oaks, CA: Corwin Press.*

Subject Area Interests and Strengths: Intermediate (Grades 4–8)

Directions: Rate the following school subjects with the appropriate number for each category. (*Teachers: Write in the subject areas or unit topics below. Students: Rate your interest level and strengths for each of these topics.*)

Interest:
(I like this topic. I'm curious about this subject. I would like to explore this topic in more depth in my spare time.)

1 = I just do not have much interest in this subject.

2 = I am sometimes interested in this subject.

3 = I am thoroughly interested in this subject.

Strength:

1 = I am not very good at this subject.

2 = I am somewhat good at this subject.

3 = I am very good at this subject.

SUBJECT/TOPICS	INTEREST	STRENGTH

Jensen, E., & Nickelsen, L. (2008). Deeper learning: 7 powerful strategies for in-depth and longer-lasting learning. *Thousand Oaks, CA: Corwin Press.*

CHAPTER 2

THE COMMON CORE STATE STANDARDS

According to the standards' authors—the National Governors Association Center for Best Practices (NGA) and the Council of Chief State School Officers (CCSSO)—the Common Core State Standards are not a curriculum. Rather,

> they are a clear set of shared goals and expectations for what knowledge and skills will help our students succeed. Local teachers, principals, superintendents and others will decide *how* the standards are to be met. Teachers will continue to devise lesson plans and tailor instruction to the individual needs of the students in their classrooms. (NGA & CCSSO, 2012a)

This chapter is all about understanding what is required for our students to achieve the ELA standards in their content area classrooms. Keep in mind that we have focused on Reading and Writing strands, but our strategies will have speaking, listening, language, and technology opportunities spread throughout. History / social studies, science, and technical teachers in grades 6–12 should note that, though they have been given special grade-level standards, they still fall under the Reading and Writing anchor standards (NGA & CCSSO, 2010; see figure I.1, page 3). These interdisciplinary standards help spread reading across all content areas.

But first, let's understand some foundational background knowledge about the CCSS.

The Basics of the CCSS

The CCSS were created to better prepare students for college and careers after high school and in our global arena. By having a shared set of national standards, U.S. educators can ensure that students in almost every state are held to the same level of expectation as students in the world's high-performing countries. The mission statement of the CCSS reads,

> The Common Core State Standards provide a consistent, clear understanding of what students are expected to learn, so teachers and parents know what they need to do to help them. The standards are designed to be robust and relevant to the real world, reflecting the knowledge and skills that our young people need for success in college and careers. With

American students fully prepared for the future, our communities will be best positioned to compete successfully in the global economy. (NGA & CCSSO, 2012c)

The standards-based education (SBE) movement was instrumental in the creation of the CCSS; prior to this movement, the textbook was the curriculum. The movement started in 1997 with California adopting the first set of clear, measurable, academic content standards. It arose out of a conviction that the expectations for all students needed to be raised. In 1999, the Public Schools Accountability Act required states that receive Title I funds to develop standards. In 2002, No Child Left Behind asked states to do the same. (See Mike Schmoker and Robert Marzano's [1999] article "Realizing the Promise of Standards-Based Education," to see the results of SBE on student achievement.) Benefits to using standards rather than textbooks include the ability to use intentional instruction with student goals in mind and having a clear progression of mastery to follow.

As you'll notice in our strategies, many 21st century skills are threaded throughout the standards, including collaboration, communication in higher manners (more speaking and writing, use of technology, and so on), critical thinking, problem solving, and complexity and rigor in the curriculum. The CCSS encourage independent thinking as well, including self-regulation skills and autonomy.

Use of 21st century skills helps our students truly be college and career ready, as required by the Common Core anchor standards. But what do college- and career-ready students look like? They demonstrate independence in the learning process (Conley, 2010). They ask questions, research the answers to those questions, and write and speak about what they are learning for various purposes, audiences, and tasks. They read a variety of texts well, even informational texts, and compare different perspectives. They form their own opinions and engage in debates and argumentative writing to support their points of view, which are formed by their persistent research. They use technology and digital media strategically during all of these cognitive processes.

According to Lucy Calkins, Mary Ehrenworth, and Christopher Lehman (2012), only 15 percent of students are performing at the level suggested by the standards. The National Assessment of Educational Progress (NAEP), given consistently across every state for decades, supports these data, showing that students' scores across the same interval have flatlined since 1992 (as cited in Calkins et al., 2012). In addition, on the Organisation for Economic Co-operation and Development's (OECD) Programme for International Student Assessment (PISA), the United States came in fourteenth out of forty-three (OECD, 2010).

The goal of the CCSS is to turn that downward trajectory around. What will this look like? Research projects will be short and focused, students will learn academic vocabulary that supports a variety of disciplines, and—most challenging—students will learn to closely read and analyze complex texts. Ideally, 70 percent of *all* reading in high school will be informational texts. Keep in mind that ELA teachers will still use a great deal of fiction while other content areas will increase the amount of nonfiction reading. In addition, 80 percent of high school writing will involve explaining and arguing about the content in complex texts. Good writing comes from good reading; appendix B of the CCSS has a list of complex books students should read (NGA & CCSSO, n.d.a).

The CCSS assessments are still being created but are expected around 2014–2015. The Partnership for Assessment of Readiness for College and Careers (PARCC) and the Smarter Balanced Assessment Consortium (SBAC) are developing assessments aligned to the CCSS. Both are funded by the U.S. Department of Education and will be administered on computers. They will be crafted to not only show what students know within their particular content areas, infused with CCSS standards, but also to show what students can do. These assessments will measure growth and college and career readiness. In addition, there will be checkpoint assessments or formative and interim test materials so teachers can take action with targeted interventions before the end-of-year test.

Where Should I Go to Learn More?

CCSS Appendix A: Research supporting key elements of the standards and glossary of terms (www .corestandards.org/assets/Appendix_A.pdf)

CCSS Appendix B: Lists of read-alouds, grade-appropriate reading books, complex texts, and genres (www.corestandards.org/assets/Appendix_B.pdf)

CCSS Appendix C: Writing samples for each grade level that meet or exceed the minimum level of proficiency for all three types: argument, informative/explanatory, and narrative (www.core standards.org/assets/Appendix_C.pdf)

The Reading & Writing Project: A collection of videos of students engaged with high-level book conversations; reading assessments; list of high-interest books (www.readingandwritingproject.com)

Student Achievement Partners: Great lessons based on the CCSS (www.achievethecore.org)

PARCC: A guide for states and districts to use while implementing the CCSS (www.parcconline.org /achieving-common-core)

SBAC: A list of resources developed to explain the standards and help teachers support student success (www.smarterbalanced.org/k-12-education/common-core-state-standards-tools-resources)

Now that we know a bit more about the CCSS, let's take a closer look at the Reading and Writing anchor standards, which are the focus for the strategies in this book.

Reading Anchor Standards

Ten college and career readiness anchor standards—organized into four domains: (1) Key Ideas and Details, (2) Craft and Structure, (3) Integration of Knowledge and Ideas, and (4) Range of Reading and Level of Text Complexity—delineate the most important concepts for the Reading strand. All ten anchor standards require deep comprehension and high-level thinking across all grade levels. As noted previously, the anchor standards are umbrella goals for all grade levels (NGA & CCSSO, 2010). Visit www.core standards.org for more information about specific grade-level standards that define what students should understand and be able to do by the end of their grade level. See appendix B (page 205) for more information about matching specific strategies to specific anchor standards.

Key Ideas and Details

The first domain in the Reading strand includes anchor standards one through three, all related to reading for meaning. We'll go through each anchor standard in order and discuss how you can incorporate these concepts in your classroom.

The first anchor standard highlights the need to read to analyze rather than just get information:

> Read closely to determine what the text says explicitly and to make logical inferences from it; cite specific textual evidence when writing or speaking to support conclusions drawn from the text. (CCRA.R.1)

This standard asks students to move from personal meaning making to rigorous analysis based on evidence from the text. Throughout the CCSS, there is an emphasis on text-centered thinking, discussing, and hypothesizing. Guide your students' discussions toward the text. For example, you could ask, "What in this text makes you think and say that?" Other examples of text-based questions include:

- What is the problem that the author is portraying?

- What contradictions do you find in the text? Why are they there, and how do they affect your understanding of the text?

- What evidence does that author use to support his or her assertions? Why? Do you agree or disagree with how he or she supported assertions?

- How is the text structured? What effect does this have on the outcome of the story or text?

- What are the key passages in the text? How do you know they are key passages?

You may have to follow up each question with: "Cite from the text."

This anchor standard, which deals with close reading, is in the spotlight more than any other standard because of its complexity and ambiguity in application with students and complex texts. In Zone 3 (page 119), we'll explore many specific strategies on this exact topic.

Reading anchor standard two deals with learning to read for overarching themes:

> Determine central ideas or themes of a text and analyze their development; summarize the key supporting details and ideas. (CCRA.R.2)

One way to help students achieve the second anchor standard is to have students stop while reading to summarize or discuss a theme in the text. This doesn't need to be done after every single paragraph unless the complexity of the text demands it. By looking at titles, subheadings, pictures, repeated words, and boldface words, students can easily identify central ideas and themes in nonfiction books.

While Reading anchor reading standard two asks students to determine and analyze the development of central ideas or themes, anchor standard three asks students to pay attention to details of interaction:

> Analyze how and why individuals, events, and ideas develop and interact over the course of a text. (CCRA.R.3)

Both standards two and three require the students to extend meaning across a whole text or story.

The grade-level skills within the Reading strands measure the same skills of understanding how different elements are introduced, developed, and concluded within a text, but the wording differs based on whether the text is informational or fictional.

Craft and Structure

Now that students have been reading for meaning, it's time to guide them into a deeper understanding of the text. This second domain, which contains Reading anchor standards four through six, will support them in this process.

Reading anchor standard four helps students' understanding of vocabulary words while reading and how the vocabulary affects the text:

> Interpret words and phrases as they are used in a text, including determining technical, connotative, and figurative meanings, and analyze how specific word choices shape meaning or tone. (CCRA.R.4)

To achieve this standard, have students pause often while reading to determine connotations (emotional meaning) of pivotal words or phrases and how they compare with the denotation (literal meaning). Students will explain how these words shaped the overall meaning and tone of what the author wrote.

Reading anchor standard five helps students take a deeper look at the author's structural choices:

> Analyze the structure of texts, including how specific sentences, paragraphs, and larger portions of the text (e.g., a section, chapter, scene, or stanza) relate to each other and the whole. (CCRA.R.5)

Once students study key words within the text, they can determine the major ways the text was structured. Ways to structure informational texts include description, problem and solution, cause and effect, chronological, compare and contrast, or a mixture of these. This standard also asks students to analyze how sentences, paragraphs, and sections of text add to the big picture. When using this standard, teachers and students focus on certain segments and how they relate and connect to the whole.

Reading anchor standard six goes deeper, asking students to pay attention to the voice and purpose of a text:

> Assess how point of view or purpose shapes the content and style of a text. (CCRA.R.6)

By stopping and reflecting during the reading process, students can focus on how the author's point of view or purpose is continually shaping the text. A next step for this standard could be to have students compare authors' perspectives and points of view.

These three anchor standards ask students to evaluate the tone, language, organization, and perspective of the author in his or her writing. Students analyze the author's decisions, and with each reading, students understand the meaning of the text in deeper ways. The next domain takes the process a step further to integrate the knowledge and ideas gleaned from the previous standards.

Integration of Knowledge and Ideas

The third domain in the Reading strand includes anchor standards seven through nine. These standards ask students to read related texts and connect and compare the ideas from these multiple perspectives.

Reading anchor standard seven encourages technology as a reading tool:

> Integrate and evaluate content presented in diverse media and formats, including visually and quantitatively, as well as in words. (CCRA.R.7)

For this standard, you could have students compare and contrast *The Hunger Games* book to the movie, *The Hunger Games* series to the *Twilight* series, or *Charlotte's Web* to *Stuart Little* (Calkins et al., 2012).

Reading anchor standard eight is focused on informational texts, not literary:

> Delineate and evaluate the argument and specific claims in a text, including the validity of the reasoning as well as the relevance and sufficiency of the evidence. (CCRA.R.8)

The goal here is for students to think deeply in order to understand precisely what the author or speaker is saying and then to question the author's assumptions and premises. According to Calkins and her colleagues (2012), when reading informational texts, "readers analyze the claims texts make, the soundness and sufficiency of their evidence, and the way a text's language and craft may reveal points of view; the emphasis is investigating ideas, claims, reasoning, and evidence, rather than themes, characters, figurative language and symbolism" (pp. 75–76). The latter focus obviously is what is required during literature reading. Both types of texts call for a higher level of analysis but with a different focus.

Reading anchor standard nine asks students to compare what texts are saying:

> Analyze how two or more texts address similar themes or topics in order to build knowledge
> or to compare the approaches the authors take. (CCRA.R.9)

Rather than comparing texts with diverse media (anchor standard seven) or with the arguments or claims made (anchor standard eight), this anchor standard focuses on comparing another text that has a similar theme or topic in order to strengthen understanding or just to compare varied approaches the authors take. For instance, if teachers provide many texts on the topic of volcanoes, students realize that each author focused on different facts about and examples of volcanoes. This could be accomplished with literature as well—students could read different types of historical fiction related to the American Revolution to broaden their understanding of the war.

Range of Reading and Level of Text Complexity

The fourth and final domain in the Reading strand includes anchor standard ten:

> Read and comprehend complex literary and informational texts independently and profi-
> ciently. (CCRA.R.10)

Do your students and the students in your school actually read a lot? Students learn to read more fluently and improve comprehension by reading high-interest, chosen texts. We need to encourage a higher level of complexity by moving students along a continual growth continuum with personal goal setting, feedback, and self-evaluation. This anchor standard is also about supporting all students with the same complex text—even if it is above their reading level. The goal is to expose *all* students to these powerful texts here and there. Sometimes they should read "just right" texts, and other times, they should be challenged tremendously with scaffolding in place.

Integration will be the key to accomplishing many of the CCSS. For instance, anchor standards one and ten can be accomplished at the same time as the other eight standards. In other words, students can closely read a complex text (which anchor standards one and ten cover) while focusing on the author's point of view or purpose in how they shape the content and style of the text (anchor standard six).

According to the document *Reading Between the Lines: What the ACT Reveals About College Readiness in Reading* (ACT, 2006), the clearest reading differentiator between students who are college ready and students who are not is the ability to comprehend complex texts. What makes a text more complex than others are the following characteristics.

> **Relationships:** Interactions among ideas or characters in the text are subtle, involved or
> deeply embedded.
>
> **Richness:** The text possesses a sizable amount of highly sophisticated information conveyed
> through data or literary devices.

Structure: The text is organized in ways that are elaborate and sometimes unconventional.

Style: The author's tone and use of language are often intricate.

Vocabulary: The author's choice of words is demanding and highly context dependent.

Purpose: The author's intent in writing the text is implicit and sometimes ambiguous. (ACT, 2006, p. 7)

Note that complex texts are both informational and literary. All of these characteristics make the brain work harder to result in meaningful connections and deeper comprehension. The CCSS website (www.core standards.org) also details how to determine what *complex* covers, including characteristics, examples for each grade level, and how to measure complexity.

As mentioned previously, the NAEP recommends a balance between literary texts and informational texts, changing with grade level (National Assessment Governing Board, 2008). In fourth grade, texts should be 50 percent literary and 50 percent informational. In other words, there should be a balance of informational texts—including history / social studies, science, and technical subject areas—and literature. In eighth grade, texts should be 45 percent literary and 55 percent informational. Finally, in twelfth grade, texts should be 30 percent literary and 70 percent informational. This means all teachers share in the responsibility of getting students reading within their content areas.

The NGA and CCSSO (2012b) concur with this new focus on informational texts:

> Fulfilling the standard for 6–12 ELA requires much greater attention to a specific category of informational text—literary nonfiction—than has been traditional. Because the ELA classroom must focus on literature (stories, drama, poetry) as well as literary nonfiction, a great deal of informational reading in grades 6–12 must take place in other classes if the NAEP assessment framework is to be matched instructionally.

The bottom line is this: more reading must occur in all classrooms with more complex informational and literary texts, but there must also be an increase in focus on informational texts. One of the goals of this book is to provide strategies that help students become successful with these complex texts, which are covered in chapter 9 (page 125).

If you want to go into more depth with the CCSS, we highly recommend reading Lucy Calkins, Mary Ehrenworth, and Chris Lehman's (2012) book *Pathways to the Common Core*. We believe it to have a strong interpretation of the standards, and it is written in an easy-to-read manner with a plethora of examples.

Reading Key Points

Following are some key points to keep in mind when considering the Reading strand anchor standards.

- The CCSS place special emphasis on students reading independently—that is, without text introductions and frontloading information about the complex text. As with all good instruction, support the students so success can occur. See the Skimming and Scanning strategy (p. 71) for more prereading ideas.

- Tim Rasinski (2010) states that fluency is one of the strongest indicators of comprehension. Accelerate students' reading progress up the ladder of text difficulty throughout the school year. Assess and document often. You can also give students short sections of grade-level complex texts to read aloud in order to check their fluency. Set goals for each student to read certain levels of books by a certain date.

- The use of scaffolding and modeling can make a big difference when preparing students for success in reading. Scaffold a reader's work by reading aloud and discussing the first chapter or first paragraph of a book, preteaching potentially difficult vocabulary during discussion, partnering same-book readers together to help one another, giving a book introduction, encouraging the reader to listen to an audio version of a challenging book and then to read it, and setting achievable reading goals with the student (Calkins et al., 2012). Do think-alouds to model good reading strategies. Have students summarize smaller sections (mark places in text where you want students to pause and recap).

- Students should be reading about the content more than the teacher lectures about the content. In fact, the teacher shouldn't be the primary source of information; students should be doing most of the thinking, speaking, reading, and writing in the classroom. That said, you should use a plethora of strategies that students can choose from in order to self-regulate their thinking and learning.

- The formative assessment process is imperative with the CCSS. First, complete a needs assessment of where students are with these standards (use running records or just give students sticky notes to jot their thoughts while reading). Next, plan your instruction so you are moving *all* students closer to each standard. Assess along the way, give them feedback, encourage self-assessment, and change instruction based on student achievement. You can learn more about the formative assessment process on a larger scale in chapter 10 (page 183).

- You and your school can create a system to evaluating and documenting student reading growth. The Reading & Writing Project (http://readingandwritingproject.com /resources/assessments/reading-assessments.html) is a great place to receive fiction and nonfiction reading assessments—running record forms—that show growth as well as which books students are able to read independently. The goal is to increase the level of each student so he or she is able to read more complex books throughout the school year.

Writing Anchor Standards

We have already learned that the new standards place a tremendous emphasis on reading. Because writing is an equal partner to reading and is key to assessing reading comprehension (Calkins et al., 2012), the standards emphasize writing too.

The Writing anchor standards are organized similarly to the Reading anchor standards in that the ten standards are organized into four domains: (1) Text Types and Purposes, (2) Production and Distribution of Writing, (3) Research to Build and Present Knowledge, and (4) Range of Writing.

Text Types and Purposes

The first domain in the Writing strand includes anchor standards one through three, all of which are related to the types of texts students will be writing and the purposes for those writings. The NAEP's writing framework expectation notes fourth graders should produce 30 percent argumentative writing, 35 percent informational, and 35 percent narrative writing (National Assessment Governing Board, 2010). Eighth graders should have 35 percent of their writing be argumentative, 35 percent informational, and 30 percent narrative. Twelfth graders should have 40 percent of their writing be argumentative, 40 percent informational, and 20 percent narrative. A 2009 ACT national curriculum survey of postsecondary instructors of composition, freshman English, and survey American literature courses found that argumentative writing was tied with informational writing as the most important types of writing needed by incoming freshmen. We'll go through each anchor standard in order and discuss several types of writing within each category.

The first Writing anchor standard is about argumentative writing.

> Write arguments to support claims in an analysis of substantive topics or texts using valid reasoning and relevant and sufficient evidence. (CCRA.W.1)

Argumentative writing can appear in reviews, persuasive essays, literary essays, op-ed columns, editorials, and essays (Calkins et al., 2012). This type of writing has three purposes: (1) to change a point of view or perspective, (2) to elicit action from the reader, or (3) to ask the reader to accept the claims and explanation of the concept, topic, or problem. When writing arguments, students will need to provide evidence from other texts in order to defend what is being said.

Argumentative writing can occur in any and all classrooms. For example, the social studies teacher can ask students to argue for or against a historical event, such as: "Do you agree or disagree that America needed to drop the bombs on Hiroshima and Nagasaki in order to end the war when we did? Support with several pieces of evidence. Be ready for someone to disagree with you." Eventually, this type of writing can bring about debates that enhance the speaking and listening sections of the CCSS. Consider visiting ThinkCERCA (http://thinkcerca.com), which is a web-based, CCSS-aligned literacy solution that prepares students for life's debatable and open-ended questions. By using ThinkCERCA's tools and content, teachers can help "students learn to read closely, think critically, and ultimately develop powerful arguments across disciplines" (ThinkCERCA, 2013).

Anchor standard two involves a form of writing that many students are familiar with—informational writing:

> Write informative/explanatory texts to examine and convey complex ideas and information clearly and accurately through the effective selection, organization, and analysis of content. (CCRA.W.2)

By the end of the twelfth grade, the CCSS expect students to write more argumentative and informational pieces than narrative. Informational writing can appear as how-to books, news or feature articles, fact sheets, literary nonfiction, blogs, websites, reports, nonfiction books, directions, recipes, lab reports, math exit tickets explaining what was learned, and so on (Calkins et al., 2012).

Informational writing gives students opportunities to convey information accurately after learning about it. The purposes of this type of writing are to increase the readers' (and writer's) knowledge of a topic, to help the readers understand a procedure or process better, and to deepen the reader's understanding of the concept. This type of writing encourages students to research their topic extensively and is powerful across the content areas: How does a black hole form? How do caterpillars become butterflies? How have the checks and balances in our government changed throughout the years? While informational writing should increase throughout the school year, the third type, narrative, actually decreases.

Writing anchor standard three is about narrative writing:

> Write narratives to develop real or imagined experiences or events using effective technique,
> well-chosen details and well-structured event sequences. (CCRA.W.3)

Narrative writing is based on students' experiences, real or imagined. This standard focuses in on details that matter (elaborations) and the correct sequencing of events, both of which are excellent skills that build on the other types of writing. Narrative writing can be expressed in several different formats, such as anecdotes, fiction, historical fiction, fantasy, narrative memoir, biography and autobiography, and narrative nonfiction (Calkins et al., 2012), and can be used for many different purposes, such as to entertain, to inform or instruct, or even to persuade.

Because a large portion of the writing occurring during ELA should be narrative, teachers in other subject areas will have a shared responsibility to incorporate the other types of writing. Now that we know the types of writing, let's explore the process of writing for these types.

Production and Distribution of Writing

The second domain in the Writing strand includes anchor standards four through six, which emphasize the various stages of the writing process.

Writing anchor standard four helps students brainstorm effectively so that all ideas are coherent with the chosen audience, purpose, and task:

> Produce clear and coherent writing in which the development, organization, and style are
> appropriate to task, purpose, and audience. (CCRA.W.4)

This piece leads to powerful writing that catches the reader's attention so he or she won't abandon the text. The writing must stay focused rather than change subjects or go off on tangents that do not return. The student must also keep the audience in mind at this stage.

Writing anchor standard five entails the writing process that teachers have been familiar with for years:

> Develop and strengthen writing as needed by planning, revising, editing, rewriting, or trying
> a new approach. (CCRA.W.5)

After students receive feedback on their writing (from peers, self, teachers, and maybe even parents), they improve the writing by taking a closer look at what they've already done. This may entail simple corrections, more involved rewriting, or even starting over in a new direction.

Once the piece is finished, the final publishing and celebration can occur with anchor standard six:

> Use technology, including the Internet, to produce and publish writing and to interact and collaborate with others. (CCRA.W.6)

This standard motivates students to complete their writing in many cases. Using technology as a publishing tool is a very engaging strategy that can enhance learning. Technology can help students present their work to the world in ways they may not have discovered before.

All three types of writing (to persuade, to inform, and to convey experience) can go through the writing process. Not all pieces of writing have to go through this longer process though; it will depend on your purpose for your students' writing. The next Writing domain gives more details on how to gather information for the three types of writing.

Research to Build and Present Knowledge

The third domain in the Writing strand includes anchor standards seven through nine, which focus on how to conduct research effectively and accurately.

Writing anchor standard seven addresses the importance of using various ways to incorporate, and reasons for incorporating, research projects into the classroom:

> Conduct short as well as more sustained research projects based on focused questions, demonstrating understanding of the subject under investigation. (CCRA.W.7)

Students will be researching in small or more grandiose ways depending on the learning outcome during particular units. The research starts with focused questions, and the common goal—no matter the length of the project—is for the student to produce work that shows understanding.

Writing anchor standard eight addresses plagiarism rules and regulations:

> Gather relevant information from multiple print and digital sources, assess the credibility and accuracy of each source, and integrate the information while avoiding plagiarism. (CCRA.W.8)

Students need to learn to search both digital and print sources for relevant material and determine if a source is credible and accurate, all while correctly citing any information used in their research.

Writing anchor standard nine deals with the importance of gleaning evidence in research sources to support the writer's purpose:

> Draw evidence from literary or informational texts to support analysis, reflection, and research. (CCRA.W.9)

As with all of the anchor standards, all content area teachers will need to embrace these standards in this research domain. This research process forces the brain to process at higher levels. Last, but certainly not least, the grand finale Writing anchor standard brings this big picture to life.

Range of Writing

The fourth and final domain in the Writing strand includes anchor standard ten, which explains that writing must become a daily habit in all classrooms for a variety of purposes:

> Write routinely over extended time frames (time for research, reflection, and revision) and shorter time frames (a single sitting or a day or two) for a range of tasks, purposes, and audiences. (CCRA.W.10)

There is a time to write extensively using a variety of sources and texts. There is a time to write a summary of what was learned in the math classroom that day on a door pass. There is a time to write to make others laugh by creating a comic or an entertaining long narrative. There is a time to go through the entire writing process and a time to skip some of the steps. There is a time to write in every classroom every single day.

Writing Key Points

Following are some key points to keep in mind when considering the Writing strand anchor standards.

- The Common Core State Standards place a tremendous emphasis on writing across all disciplines. Writing should become a habit. These standards are to be a shared responsibility among all disciplines and every teacher.

- Appendix C on the CCSS website (NGA & CCSSO, n.d.b) has many examples of the high proficiency levels required by the CCSS. Share these exemplars with students so they see the goal.

- Types of writing include arguments (reviews, persuasive essays, literary essays, op-ed columns, editorials, essays); informative/explanatory (how-to books, news or feature articles, fact sheets, literary nonfiction, blogs, websites, reports, nonfiction books, directions, recipes, lab reports); and narratives (personal, fiction, historical fiction, fantasy, narrative memoir, biography, narrative nonfiction).

- One writing program that has been promoted to support the CCSS is the Reading & Writing Project.

- Teachers should include short and long research projects that draw evidence from texts.

- Technology should be used to produce and publish writing pieces and to interact and collaborate with others.

Now that we've looked at the Reading and Writing strands, let's take a quick peek into the other two ELA strands, which we'll touch on every once in a while when looking at strategies.

Speaking and Listening and Language Anchor Standards

The six anchor standards in the Speaking and Listening strand require students to acquire, evaluate, and present increasingly complex information, ideas, concepts, and evidence through listening and speaking as well as through media. Though we do not directly deal with these standards often in this book, they do connect with the Reading and Writing strands.

Prepare for and participate effectively in a range of conversations and collaborations with diverse partners, building on others' ideas and expressing their own clearly and persuasively. (CCRA.SL.1)

Integrate and evaluate information presented in diverse media and formats, including visually, quantitatively, and orally. (CCRA.SL.2)

Evaluate a speaker's point of view, reasoning, and use of evidence and rhetoric. (CCRA.SL.3)

Present information, findings, and supporting evidence such that listeners can follow the line of reasoning and the organization, development, and style are appropriate to task, purpose, and audience. (CCRA.SL.4)

Make strategic use of digital media and visual displays of data to express information and enhance understanding of presentations. (CCRA.SL.5)

Adapt speech to a variety of contexts and communicative tasks, demonstrating command of formal English when indicated or appropriate. (CCRA.SL.6)

Connections between the Speaking and Listening strand and the Reading and Writing strands include presenting topics that we read and write about accurately and effectively, using proper grammar and formal English, using technology to express what we have learned through our reading and writing, using the argumentative writing pieces to discuss whether or not the claims were supported with appropriate evidence (debates, Socratic seminars, or conversations), and discussing in small groups what was read or written. We love this set of standards because it asks students to share verbally and listen intently about the learning that has occurred.

These standards focus on academic discussion in one-on-one, small-group, and whole-class settings, which can be accomplished through flexibly or purposefully grouping students. Such discussions can be achieved through formal presentations with rubrics of expectations or informally when students collaborate to answer questions or solve problems.

Students' vocabularies are grown through a mix of conversations, direct instruction, reading, and writing. The six Language anchor standards, which we do not deal directly with in this text, help students determine word meanings (connotative and denotative), appreciate the nuances of words, progressively expand their repertoire of words and phrases, and creatively express themselves through language.

Demonstrate command of the conventions of standard English grammar and usage when writing or speaking. (CCRA.L.1)

Demonstrate command of the conventions of standard English capitalization, punctuation, and spelling when writing. (CCRA.L.2)

Apply knowledge of language to understand how language functions in different contexts, to make effective choices for meaning or style, and to comprehend more fully when reading or listening. (CCRA.L.3)

Determine or clarify the meaning of unknown and multiple-meaning words and phrases by using context clues, analyzing meaningful word parts, and consulting general and specialized reference materials, as appropriate. (CCRA.L.4)

Demonstrate understanding of figurative language, word relationships, and nuances in word meanings. (CCRA.L.5)

Acquire and use accurately a range of general academic and domain-specific words and phrases sufficient for reading, writing, speaking, and listening at the college and career readiness level; demonstrate independence in gathering vocabulary knowledge when encountering an unknown term important to comprehension or expression. (CCRA.L.6)

These standards can be integrated with and assessed through Speaking and Listening standards as well as Writing standards. Technology practices are also integrated throughout the Writing, Reading, and Speaking and Listening strands. For example, Reading anchor standard seven says: "Integrate and evaluate content presented in diverse media and formats, including visually and quantitatively, as well as in words" (CCRA.R.7).

Conclusion

Willona Sloan (2010), writing about the history behind and implementation of the Common Core State Standards, notes,

> The National Center for Educational Achievement and ACT, Inc. (Montgomery & Mercado, 2010) suggest what it will take for the Common Core standards to succeed: "Belief that all students can reach the standards and the educator behaviors to support it. Coherent support structures from state-level down to classroom-level. Willingness and awareness that this is just the first and necessary step . . . The key is in the implementation."

Thus the rest of this book explains *how* to implement these ELA standards throughout every subject area. It is the responsibility of all teachers in all content areas to facilitate reading and writing skills with all of their students. Study the tables in appendix B (page 205) to see how this book's strategies support the anchor standards.

Because the CCSS have much higher expectations than most states are used to, cognitive engagement is a must when creating strategies to meet these standards. The next chapter dives into organizing the standards into the three successive engagement zones.

ASQ Time

1. **Action step:** What is the single most valuable next step you will take after having read this chapter?

2. **Summary of learning:** Summarize in three to five sentences what you learned in this chapter.

3. **Question:** What discussion questions do you have for other readers, for the authors, or for self-reflection to explore more from this chapter?

CHAPTER 3

HOW TO TURN STANDARDS INTO TARGETS

How can teachers engage students in every lesson? By planning for it. No planning means no success. This chapter will help you understand the three engagement zones, determine the most appropriate engagement zone for each of your students, and build a standard-based target within that zone. We want to make this process as easy as possible.

The Three Engagement Zones

We created the following zones after studying many taxonomies for thinking such as the revised version of Benjamin Bloom's Taxonomy, Norman Webb's Depth of Knowledge, and Art Costa's Three-Story Intellect. Cognitive engagement has numerous verbs to describe it: *creating, discussing, debating, assimilating, synthesizing, analyzing,* and so on. You have seen these verbs before—possibly in Bloom's Taxonomy (Anderson & Krathwohl, 2001). Because most teachers are familiar with Bloom's Taxonomy and because it best explains different categories of thinking, we simplified and synthesized his six categories of thinking into the following three categories.

Zone 1: Engage to Build Basics—This zone allows students to explain in simple terms what they know or are learning at the time in order to build basic background knowledge or to prime the brain for future learning. They can define, explain partially, draw, and start to wonder about their learning. It's a great introductory lesson for a standard; their brains will become oriented with the topic.

Zone 2: Engage to Explore—This zone creates explorers in the classroom, students who want to learn more. They generate questions, compare the learning to other concepts they know, sort content, research, and make personal connections with the content.

Zone 3: Engage to Own—This zone cognitively engages students at the ownership level, where they apply the content to benefit others, transfer the knowledge to other disciplines, scrutinize texts to challenge authors and students' own beliefs, and even want to create something new after learning about it. When students enter this zone, watch out; they tend to think outside the box and want to share what they came up with.

This is critical, so read this twice: *The Common Core State Standards are asking us to take students past Engage to Build Basics and on to the Engage to Explore and Engage to Own zones.* We must build the basics *before* we get students exploring and owning content. If we teach the basic information smarter, we have more time to take students to the higher levels of critical thinking. We have two chapters full of ideas dedicated to each of these cognitive thinking levels. Each zone will have the following ideas ready to plug into your lessons:

- Questions and question stems for you and for your students to ask and answer within the lesson

- Strategies to support the engagement zone

- A preparations and materials list for each strategy

- Instructions for each strategy

- Assessment ideas for each strategy to get students to demonstrate and share their learning with others in the school and community

Use table 3.1 to build the basics; it explains other descriptors for the zones, examples of how students can think in these zones, how to know when to use certain zones in a lesson, and which strategies support which zone.

We want to make sure that we all have some basic assumptions in mind when planning within each zone. The following pieces should exist in every lesson or engagement zone:

- Just because you are teaching within a particular zone doesn't mean you can't take your students to other zones during that lesson. The primary zone you are taking your students toward depends on how you are asking your students to think during the lesson. Remember, the target is what all students are trying to achieve. Your questions, assessments, and strategies should help students get there.

- Differentiation should occur within all of the zones. See appendix A (page 197) for a list of great ways to differentiate for your students so they learn in their special way. The strategies you choose from this extensive list should be based on your students' needs, so get to know those kids well.

- In all zones, students—rather than teachers—should be doing most of the thinking and acting. This book is going to help you choose questions, activities, and assessments to keep your students engaged all day long. The CCSS are all about students becoming more independent learners; these strategies promote that independence.

- While some students might need to go through the scaffolding of the Engage to Explore Zone before starting the Engage to Own Zone, many will not. Because both zones promote higher-level thinking, you do not necessarily have to engage students in Zone 2: Engage to Explore before engaging them in Zone 3.

Once you've decided which engagement zone is best for each of your students, you'll need to turn your chosen standard into a target. We'll first discuss the various pieces of this progression and then walk through the entire process with a specific target in mind.

Designing a Three-Step Target

Every lesson needs a specific target formed from a broad standard. At this point, your state should have a list of CCSS-friendly, grade-level specific standards for all of your subject areas. From these broad standards,

Table 3.1: A Quick Look at the Three Engagement Zones

ZONE 1: ENGAGE TO BUILD BASICS (basic, new, introductory, simple)		
After Experiencing This Zone	**When to Use This Zone**	**Strategies or Activities to Support the Zone**

Students should be able to:
 	
• Explain what was learned in simple terms
• Define words learned
• Match ideas
• Recall rote learning (facts, lists)
• Draw a picture
• Share basic information or processes
• Share what they know on a topic
• Respond with wonder and awe at a few of the facts
	When you are
	(or when the standard is):
	
	• Introducing a new topic
	• Finding out what students know
	• Giving them a short, easy-to-read text about your topic
	• Asking them to give you basic or beginner information about the topic
	• Priming their brain for the next unit
	• Activating their prior knowledge
	• Asking them to define or explain vocabulary terms
	• Reviewing or recalling what was already learned
	• Identifying problems
	• Sharing a website or explaining new technology
		Chapter 5 (page 55)
		
		1. Pre-Exposure and Priming
		  • Treasure Chest of Artifacts
		  • Book Tagging
		  • Ultimate Bulletin Board
		  • Your Ticket In
		  • IDEA Vocabulary Organizer
		2. *The Important Book*
		3. Historical Event Web
		4. Kinesthetic Vocabulary
		5. Super Sleuth
		6. Activating Prior Knowledge Dice
		7. List-Sort-Label-Write
		8. Carousel Brainstorm
		9. Skimming and Scanning
		10. Reporter Goes Big Time

ZONE 2: ENGAGE TO EXPLORE (question, wonder, grapple with, imagine, spark)		
After Experiencing This Zone	**When to Use This Zone**	**Strategies or Activities to Support the Zone**
Students should be able to: • Generate questions • Compare information to something they already know or have experienced • Sort words or objects into similar categories • Make connections with content and among other disciplines • Make content more relevant to his or her personal life • Create analogies, similes, and metaphors for the learning • Research a topic of interest to find out answers to questions or to support opinions	When you are (or when the standard is): • Encouraging students to generate questions on the topic • Wanting students to get creative with content, to imagine, to wonder • Connecting previous background knowledge with new background knowledge • Asking students to compare and contrast information • Incorporating more meaning with the content; connecting it personally with the students' experiences or knowledge • Wanting students to get excited and want to learn more about the content or skill • Asking students to dive deeply into content by researching it	Chapter 7 (page 93) 11. The Big 6 Research Process 12. Produce, Improve, Prioritize 13. Brainstorming Bonanza 14. Finding Credible and Accurate Resources 15. Speak What You Know 16. Quad Cards 17. Reflective Conversations 18. H Diagram 19. Stump the Chump

Continued →

ZONE 3: ENGAGE TO OWN
(apply, transfer learning, take action, serve, design)

After Experiencing This Zone	When to Use This Zone	Strategies or Activities to Support the Zone
Students should be able to: · Apply newly learned skills to the classroom assignment and in different contexts · Use the content to create a solution · Get others involved in order to implement a plan of action · Apply information at the personal, local, national, or international level · Decide how this information can benefit others · Change the content into a different form (from picture or graphic to writing, from writing to speaking, from direct quote to paraphrase) · Create their own theory and be able to support it · Debate or share opinions with support on a topic · Explain, summarize, or paraphrase using additional ideas from themselves or other sources · Use higher-level vocabulary words correctly to express the learning · Set goals for future learning · Empathize with situations and others' perspectives · Listen with understanding and empathy and then summarize what was said · Think about their own thinking; explain their thinking processes	When you are (or when the standard is): · Solving real problems within the world, community or school, personal homes, or classroom · Predicting how the world might respond to certain actions · Needing the students to demonstrate a skill or process · Asking students to invent something for the benefit of specific locations · Wanting them to apply what they know to a new situation · Assisting students with the transfer of the knowledge into a new context · Creating new ideas and applying them · Asking students to closely read challenging text and go deeper into the text's meaning	Chapter 9 (page 125) 22. Close Reading Steps 21. Close Reading Marks 22. Three Short Summaries for Nonfiction 23. Fix-It Activities 24. Reciprocal Teaching With Nonfiction 25. Mindmapping for Solutions 26. Stop-n-Think 27. Interactive Notebook 28. Walking in the Shoes of Another 29. Six Thinking Hats 30. Socratic Seminars

you create the specific, daily targets that can be measured within the one to three days spent teaching the lesson. (Some daily lesson targets could take up to three days to teach fully.) Targets have three requirements:

1. **Do—The thinking verb.** What will students actually *do* within this lesson? This verb choice will determine the rigor and length of the strategy, thus defining which engagement zone the target will fall into.

2. **Know—Specific content they should know for this lesson**. What do your standards tell you that they should master? This is very specific and can be measured in one to three days as compared to a broad standard measured after many days of detailed lessons.

3. **Show—The result.** How will the students prove they Do and Know? We give the students the specific criteria for success for this assessment product. The criteria clearly define what is expected in the Do and Know so students know exactly what is needed to show they mastered this target.

The Do

Every target needs a powerful verb to show how the students will be thinking. Most importantly, this verb determines which engagement zone you will use to plan in your lesson. For a list of verbs from each zone, see the following pages: Zone 1, page 52; Zone 2, page 91; Zone 3, page 122. If your verbs are consistently in the lowest cognitive engagement zone (Zone 1: Engage to Build Basics), then you will need to revise some of your targets, because the CCSS ask students to think at higher levels. Yes, our students do need simple learning, but the majority of our lessons should be focused on depth. How will you ask your students to *think* about what they are to learn?

Some thinking verbs and phrases that the CCSS emphasize are:

- Reasoning within texts and giving evidence

- Considering and evaluating different viewpoints and perspectives based on evidence

- Building theories based on evidence

- Creating interpretations based on evidence

- Interpreting words and phrases and analyzing how they relate to one another or to certain events or concepts

- Analyzing the structure of a text

- Integrating and evaluating content from a variety of formats

- Delineating and evaluating the validity of arguments and their claims

When we plan our Do and Know, we plan them simultaneously. You can't choose a verb without knowing the specific content students must learn. They go hand-in-hand. Some teachers start with: "Students will know . . ." and place the content with it. This will lead to lower-level, simple learning if done the majority of the time. There is a time for simple learning targets, but why not bump up the verb level so students are doing more than acquiring information?

The Know

The Know is the content. It should come directly from the standard itself. You may need to collaborate with other teachers to extract the specific daily content needs from the standard. When creating specific targets, we would sit with our colleagues and decide through a task analysis which daily targets would get students to the big standard. Many state curricula have created the specific daily targets, objectives, or outcomes (each state calls these goals something different).

The Show

The Show is the result. It has two pieces: (1) the criteria for success and (2) the product. The criteria for success are provided first to help ensure that students know exactly what is expected with the product. They can be a checklist of requirements, a rubric of expectations, an exemplar (showing students a good and poor example so they can see the difference), questions, or a self-assessment. When the criteria for success are in place, students can self-regulate their learning.

The product gives you and your students evidence of the learning. It is what you hear or see that tells you that they got it or didn't get it. It could be as simple as a journal entry or as complex as a Socratic seminar. Some familiar examples include graphic organizers, notes, interactive notebooks, mindmaps, debates, speeches, writing, answers to questions, and so on.

Let's review the overall structure of information in order to move from a standard to a target. Figure 3.1 explains how to quickly plan the most engaging targets for your students.

You begin with the big standard chosen from the CCSS. Next, through Do, Know, and Show, you create a specific target. The verb you choose in the Do step determines which engagement zone the students will be working in.

Next, pick question stems listed in chapter 4 (Zone 1), chapter 6 (Zone 2), or chapter 8 (Zone 3) to help your students begin thinking within the context of the correct zone. Then, choose a strategy from chapter 5 (Zone 1), chapter 7 (Zone 2), or chapter 9 (Zone 3) to engage students and help them achieve your target. Finally, choose—or have students choose—a way to assess their product (the Show) based on the criteria of success you provided them. Now that you know how to build a target from a standard, we'll walk through the entire process with a sample standard.

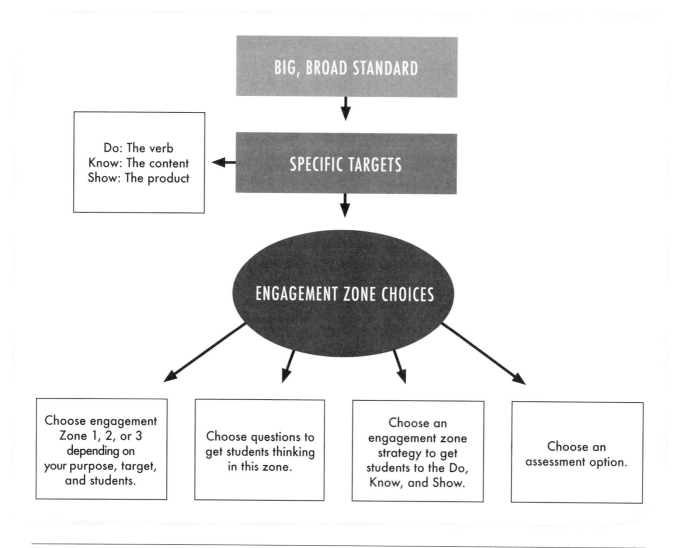

Figure 3.1: The engagement zone big picture.

Standard-to-Target Walkthrough

Let's start with a fifth-grade science standard about ecosystems. The broad standard is: "Students will understand the interdependence of plants and animals with their ecosystem."

We need to break this standard into smaller, attainable daily learning targets so we can check for progress toward the goal; it will take multiple detailed daily lessons to get students to this standard. One target to get students to this standard could be: "The students will compare and contrast the common ecosystems such as estuaries and salt marshes; oceans and ponds; or forests and grasslands by completing an H diagram between two of these terms." This target is in Zone 2 because *compare* and *contrast* are more involved verbs.

Let's break this down into the three essential parts of a great target.

1. **Do:** Read articles with chosen terms, create a list of characteristics, and then compare and contrast in an essay (to inform).

2. **Know:** Understand characteristics of estuaries versus salt marshes; oceans versus ponds; or forests versus grasslands.

3. **Show:** Fill in an H diagram with two of the terms (see strategy 18, page 107, for an example) and write an essay about the similarities and differences between these two terms.

The criteria for success might be a student-and-teacher-generated checklist of what is expected on the H diagram and how students will share their learning with the class.

Notice that to attain the content, students are directed to read nonfiction rather than listen to the teacher teach the content. The teacher will, however, be explicitly teaching the vocabulary to each group based on the article choice. While reading, students record a list of the characteristics for their choice of terms. Then they engage in rich discussion and questions from the teacher and classmates to broaden their understanding of what was read and written.

The next step is for students to create their H diagrams. Once the diagrams are completed, students can present their essays and share their H diagrams. This activity can promote higher-level thinking with many extensions to help students achieve the rigorous ELA anchor standards.

See the feature boxes on pages 38 and 39 for two grade-level examples of implementing the three-step daily target.

Self-Assessment

A very important part of students engaging in targets that require higher-level thinking is self-assessment. Rick Stiggins and Jan Chappuis (2005), two assessment gurus, discovered the empowering effects of student self-assessment and summarized it in their article "Using Student-Involved Classroom Assessment to Close Achievement Gaps," yet many classrooms aren't using it to its full advantage. They write that student responsibility for learning can be achieved most effectively by consciously involving students in the assessment process. Students should be involved in designing or selecting assessment strategies, developing criteria, keeping records of their achievement, and communicating about their learning (Stiggins & Chappuis, 2005).

The CCSS promote independent learning by encouraging higher-level thinking supported by evidence and having students both determine where they are with the standards and choose strategies to help them successfully learn content in deeper ways. When we get students involved in the assessment process, there is more buy-in, motivation to perform better, and higher achievement in the classroom (Black & Wiliam, 1998b). In his article "Formative Assessment and the Design of Instructional Systems," D. Royce Sadler (1989) states that in order for students to improve, they should have the capacity to monitor the quality of their work toward the target during the actual production. This requires the learner to do the following three things: (1) understand what the target is, (2) compare the current level of performance with this target, and (3) then engage in the appropriate action to fully achieve the target. When teachers use the strategies in this book, it will be crucial for students to self-assess.

First-Grade Language Arts

Standard: Ask and answer questions about key details in a text.

Do: Ask and answer questions (*ask* is a Zone 2 verb since it involves generating questions based on details gathered).

Know: Understand key details in the informational text *Garden Helpers* (National Geographic Society, 2009).

Show: Create a T-chart with questions and detailed answers.

Target: Students will ask and answer questions by writing key details from the text *Garden Helpers* in the form of a T-chart.

Write this target in first person on the dry-erase board for students to see what is expected: "I can ask and answer questions by writing key details in a T-chart." Then give students examples of what key details look like. Find key details and place them on the T-chart together with a section of the book, and then ask them to do one with a partner. Ask them to self-assess their level of understanding of this target with a thumbs-up, thumb in the middle, or thumbs-down. Eventually, when you see that they are ready, ask them to complete one question and answer pair on the T-chart on their own and check for understanding.

Criteria for success: There are a variety of questions written on the left-hand side of the "T"; answers are text-based and written across from the question on the right side of the "T"; answers show understanding of the article; students used the question stems to help create the questions.

Differentiation options: Pull out a small group of struggling readers with you to guide them with reading the complex text; use chart paper together to guide the T-chart conversation; copy the section of text for them so they can highlight important details with you.

Lynn S. Fuchs and Douglas Fuchs (1986) say that when some students graphically display their achievement (monitor their progress with daily learning goals) there is a 26 percentile point gain in achievement. Students can start the process tomorrow with the following simple activities. See pages 41–46 for reproducible versions of these activities or visit **go.solution-tree.com/commoncore** to download them.

- **Daily Stoplights (Elementary):** Give this form to your students with the targets for the week already written out. Choose whatever your students need the most support in; for instance, you might select just math targets for this form. Sometime during or after the lesson, ask your students to determine where their work is compared to the target and criteria for success. Students then color in the stoplight. A red light means they aren't yet accomplishing the target goal, a yellow light means they need more practice with the target, and a green light means they understand and have achieved the target. Have students explain the color they chose in the comments box (this could just be a verbal explanation too). The next step is to give feedback to help students determine how the gap will be closed and how they will proceed to accomplish the target.

Middle School Social Studies

Standard: Analyze the impact of major conflicts, battles, and wars on the development of our nation.

Do: Evaluate loyalist or patriot perspectives (*evaluate* is a Zone 3 word).

Know: Understand six turning points (positive or negative) of the Revolutionary War (battles, events, and writings).

Show: Create a point-of-view timeline and a final written analysis from the perspective chosen.

Target: Students will be able to evaluate, from the loyalist or patriot perspective, six turning points within the Revolutionary War by creating a point-of-view timeline and writing an accompanying analysis.

This lesson wraps up a unit on the Revolutionary War and should take about three days to complete. Students will be reading through the many texts they were exposed to during the unit in order to create this timeline. They will also be reading about the points of view on the war through the lenses of a loyalist or patriot. Different texts highlighted different perspectives on the war, so students will be engaging with Reading anchor standard six in order to complete the timeline as well as most of the Writing anchor standards when working on perspective. (See pages 20–28 for a list of Reading and Writing anchor standards).

Criteria for success: Show exemplars of the point-of-view timeline from a different historical era; have students list what made this example so stellar; create a rubric for the timeline and written analysis.

Differentiation options: Form a small group of struggling students (those who can't get started or still don't understand the difference between a loyalist and patriot) and help learners begin by showing a T-chart of the differences between the loyalists and patriots. Then help them brainstorm turning points in the war that affected the groups. Finally, assist them in taking on the perspective of a loyalist or patriot and determining if the turning points were positive or negative (also show students how to rate these events). They might need an outline of how to write the analysis as well.

- **Daily Targets (Elementary):** Choose a subject that, based on data, your students are struggling with. Have students write the target in the designated spot on the form, and sometime during or after the lesson, ask the students to determine where their work is compared to the target and the criteria for success. Students should place an *X* on the bull's-eye to show the level of mastery or understanding. Students then explain in the next box why their work is not at the bull's-eye yet (obviously, if a student believes the work is in the bull's-eye, he or she will skip this box). Next, give feedback to the students to help them determine how the gap will be closed and how they will proceed to accomplish the target. The goal is to get students into one engagement zone per lesson. If they are experiencing one or more of the activities within that zone, they should be engaged cognitively. The decisions you have to make include: What zone do I want my students within during the lesson? What is the desired target—what do I want to see and hear when the lesson is over?

- **My Progress Learning Graph (Grades 4–8):** This graph is a little less time consuming than the two previously listed. Students simply write the target in the bottom slanted lines and color in or graph the level of mastery after the lesson. All good curricula bring those targets back often, and good teachers reteach in a different way until students reach the target. Give students multiple opportunities to color the graph to the top. What a powerful visual for growth!

- **Weekly Progress Monitoring (Grades 6–8):** This form is quite popular in middle and high schools since classes almost always start with a warm-up. Students should document how they did on the warm-up after it is discussed. Then teachers share the target for the day and students write it. Toward the end of class, ask the students to get this form out again to record the outcome; they answer the closure question or solve the problem that directly relates to the target in the last box. Finally, as students leave, they document their door pass response. This assessment serves as the warm-up, self-evaluation, and door pass for each student at the beginning of the class and end of the class all in one form!

Another type of assessment tool that comes in handy in collecting daily data from your students is documenting what you are seeing and hearing. This can be done by walking around the room and jotting down symbols that represent where the students are with the target that day; all that is really needed is a symbol of mastery. This can be done quickly and easily with a Cruisin' Clipboard (page 47 or visit **go.solution -tree.com/commoncore** to download). After a formative assessment (dry-erase, show-me boards, door pass, electronic voting, sample writing, and so on), you can do a quick check with certain students or with all students. The most important piece to this documentation is using the data to change your instruction so that students can get to the target. The Cruisin' Clipboard has a list of ways to change your instruction if needed. You should always take action when students are not getting the target. The form also allows you to mark a response code that documents how you took care of the situation.

Each of the thirty strategies in the following chapters will have assessment ideas for you to choose from. In addition, the engaging lesson plan template in chapter 10 (page 184) lists criteria for success that you can use in your daily targets.

Conclusion

We hope that student self-assessment will become very powerful in your classroom. This large, empowering step toward more independent students is a foundational desire in the CCSS, and it is a powerful engagement strategy.

The next two chapters will explore Zone 1: Engage to Build Basics. Zone 1 helps you prepare your students for the higher-level thinking that the CCSS require. You will learn to build their background knowledge in smarter ways so they can think critically about the new concepts learned.

ASQ Time

1. **Action step:** What is the single most valuable next step you will take after having read this chapter?

2. **Summary of learning:** Summarize in three to five sentences what you learned in this chapter.

3. **Question:** What discussion questions do you have for other readers, for the authors, or for self-reflection to explore more from this chapter?

Daily Stoplights Student Self-Assessment

Name: _____

Subject: _____ Unit: _____

TARGET	COMMENTS
Monday Target:	Why did you choose that color?
Tuesday Target:	Why did you choose that color?
Wednesday Target:	Why did you choose that color?

page 1 of 2

Bringing the Common Core to Life in K–8 Classrooms ©2014 Solution Tree Press • solution-tree.com
Visit **go.solution-tree.com/commoncore** to download this page.

TARGET	COMMENTS
Thursday Target:	Why did you choose that color?
Friday Target:	Why did you choose that color?

Conference with teacher notes (goals for review):

Daily Targets Student Self-Assessment

Name: _____

Subject: _____ Unit: _____

TARGET	COMMENTS
Monday Target: Got It! Need More Practice Not Yet	Why did you place the X in that particular location? Demonstrate your learning today:
Tuesday Target: Got It! Need More Practice Not Yet	Why did you place the X in that particular location? Demonstrate your learning today:
Wednesday Target: Got It! Need More Practice Not Yet	Why did you place the X in that particular location? Demonstrate your learning today:

TARGET	COMMENTS
Thursday Target: — Got It! — Need More Practice — Not Yet	Why did you place the *X* in that particular location? Demonstrate your learning today:
Friday Target: — Got It! — Need More Practice — Not Yet	Why did you place the *X* in that particular location? Demonstrate your learning today:

Conference with teacher notes (goals for review):

My Progress Learning Graph

Name: _____ Subject Area: _____

GOT IT										
MORE PRACTICE										
APPROACHING										
NOT YET										

Date and
Outcomes

Weekly Progress Monitoring

DAY OF WEEK	WARM-UP		OUTCOME	DOOR PASS RESPONSE	
Monday		Got It			Got It
		More			More
		Not Yet			Not Yet
Tuesday		Got It			Got It
		More			More
		Not Yet			Not Yet
Wednesday		Got It			Got It
		More			More
		Not Yet			Not Yet
Thursday		Got It			Got It
		More			More
		Not Yet			Not Yet
Friday		Got It			Got It
		More			More
		Not Yet			Not Yet

Cruisin' Clipboard Documentation

Subject: _____ Unit: _____ Date: _____

Level of Mastery (LOM) Key

+   Advanced

✓   Got It

-    More Practice

- -   Not Yet

Response (Res.) Key

FG = Flexible groups (small groups of students with same readiness level, interest level, or learning preference—homogeneous groups OR small groups of students with different readiness levels, interest levels, or learning preferences—heterogeneous)

1o1 = One on one (reteaching or extending a concept with just one student and you, the teacher)

VAK = Different modality (visual, auditory, and kinesthetic)

S = Spiral back in (come back to this target another time)

R = Reteach (retaught the target in a different way; could be one on one or in small group or whole class depending on what was observed)

SS = Scaffold strategies (gradually release the responsibility given to student to perform the task or learn the content depending on what student needs)

	STUDENT LEARNING TARGET:			STUDENT LEARNING TARGET:			STUDENT LEARNING TARGET:		
Student	LOM	Notes	Res.	LOM	Notes	Res.	LOM	Notes	Res.

page 2 of 2

CHAPTER 4

ZONE 1: ENGAGE TO BUILD BASICS

LeAnn will never forget when her sixth-grade teacher made the whole class memorize all the world's countries along with their capitals and locations. Students played weekly games and studied one continent at a time. Though her semantic memory sure did get a workout that year, she's now thankful for the learning experience. Those opportunities to build foundational background knowledge of geography helped her understand the evening news much better. She can now visualize where those countries are and who borders them. Such surface-level learning is common for this initial zone. It's not a waste of time at all; it helps prime the brain and build the background for later learning.

Zone 1: Engage to Build Basics is where it all begins, the bellwether to the other zones. It can also be called the introductory or entry zone. People who have spent a lot of time in this zone should be successful with games such as *Jeopardy!* and Trivial Pursuit, as it's the fact-gathering step in learning. This zone covers building background knowledge (hooking students and making them more curious with snippets of facts about your topic) as well as activating prior knowledge (activating information that has become part of them from previous learning and experiences).

The level or quality of student background knowledge has a lot to do with his or her achievement, since the child's schema provides the platform vocabulary needed to succeed (Zull, 2002). If students don't have sufficient background knowledge to build on, you will need to integrate the missing chunks of information into your instruction with scaffolding. There's a good reason to do this: what students already know and how they have performed on the subject is one of the strongest indicators of how well they will learn new information about it. In fact, it ranks a powerful 0.67 effect size (Hattie, 2009), which places it in the top 20 percent of all achievement factors. In the world of research, you'll often hear the phrase *effect size* used. An effect size is simply a standardized measure of the effect that one agent has on student achievement. While it's possible to have negative effect sizes, most fall between 0.00 and 0.40. Effect sizes falling under 0.20 are considered trivial. Those from 0.20 to 0.40 are considered moderate. Any effect size from 0.40 to 2.0 is considered very significant.

Thus the art of activating prior knowledge is equally imperative to building that background knowledge in the first place. There are several engaging ways to activate prior knowledge, such as through questions and answers, small-group discussion or games, and writing.

Beyond improving how well students will learn, there are also several other reasons to secure a strong foundation through building background knowledge and activating prior knowledge (Jensen & Nickelsen, 2008):

- To improve opportunities for memory of the concepts or skills taught

- To cultivate the connections so relevancy can occur

- To ensure that students' background knowledge has a strong foundation

- To correct students' misconceptions

- To foster interest, motivation, and excitement

How important is this zone in relation to the other zones? Analyzing and thinking critically require the extensive factual knowledge this zone provides. The better we facilitate Zone 1, the more time we have to take our students through the other zones. Teaching smarter includes helping students get these rote facts and skills quickly into their long-term memory so they can use them for exploring and thinking critically about these concepts in relation to the many others stored in their brains. It also includes using the most powerful, efficient memory strategies to get more bang for your buck. In addition, teaching smarter with the CCSS prepares students' brains before reading and writing. This chapter will explain how to teach smarter rather than harder.

Jumpstarting the Brain

Brains get exposed to information all the time. The first potential barrier to storing long-term memories is our safety filters. We are aroused by danger, contrast, risk, and novelty. These experiences are initially processed by our fast-responding early warning structures that tell us to fight, freeze, or take flight. If danger is not an issue, then the brain can attend to content, especially the executive function skills (Lindström & Bohlin, 2012).

To get students ready, make the environment safe, build relationships, and *then* get them to care about the content. Once each student cares or is invested in your topic, building the basics gets much easier. New explicit information (concepts, terms, definitions, insights, summaries, facts, and so on) is held for a few seconds in our working memory. These representations are either aural (lecture, podcast) or visual (website, poster, drawing, book page) (Loomis, Klatzky, McHugh, & Giudice, 2012). Every student has various capacity levels of working memory. While memory capacity can be strengthened, working memory is the first entry point for new learning (McGettigan et al., 2011; Rutman, Clapp, Chadick, & Gazzaley, 2010).

The content in our working memory is then either deleted or moved to the next stage—the hippocampus. This *C*-shaped structure is located midbrain, and it stores or catalogues information temporarily until it decides (mostly at night, while we're sleeping) to either delete the information or to go ahead and move the memories into long-term memory in our cortex. The hippocampus is highly engaged when new connections are made and new memories of content are formed. It takes much effort to keep information in this semantic memory center. In other words, to really know this information, students need to grapple with it over time. That is why taking students to the next two zones is of great importance—these are where meaning and lasting memory can occur.

To recap, the steps for solid learning are, first, to get the brain's attention and transfer the information into the working memory; second, to move it to the hippocampus to create connections; and third, to then make the information meaningful enough to get moved to permanent storage in the cortex. Thus, a well-written question can become a pivotal point in a lesson. When a compelling question is asked, the brain pays attention to it more than it would just a statement. In fact, powerful questions can evoke anticipation, curiosity, and intrigue. They can stimulate the brain into waiting and wanting to find out the answer. We should always include well-crafted questions that steer students toward the learning goal in every lesson. Here are some questions and question stems that might help you plan for Zone 1:

- Were you surprised that _____?
- What do you know about _____?
- Can you solve the puzzle of _____?
- Can you define, list, recall, or identify _____?
- How would you explain this mystery?
- How would you describe _____?
- How did _____ happen?
- Can you explain what is meant by _____?
- Are you aware of how you responded to _____?
- What background or biases have shaped your awareness?
- How do you know what you know?
- Are you sure enough to bet on _____?
- How reliable and valid is _____?
- What do you mean?
- What do you think is going on here?
- Do you believe we have enough facts to suggest _____?
- What are the core (or unusual) features, parts, characteristics, or properties of _____?

The greater the prior knowledge, the easier and faster the learning—*if* the new learning is compatible with the old. If the new information is contrary to prior knowledge, then the existing neural networks can become a significant obstacle that should not be underestimated. New approaches and constant revision of learning are necessary (Jensen & Nickelsen, 2008). In short, prior knowledge is far more significant of an influence (good or bad) than most educators acknowledge.

Each strategy in this zone will build students' background knowledge for target mastery (see chapter 5, page 55, for all Zone 1 strategies). Read through all of them to determine which will help your students with your particular target. They have been designed to work with almost any content to build background knowledge in small, snippet-like manners so that when the bigger chunks of information come, the brain will have a familiar neural network to snuggle next to. The CCSS take students to great depths, and simple background knowledge will be needed to prepare for the deeper thinking.

When to Use Zone 1

You will want to use the strategies, questions, and assessments from this zone when your target is focused on the following:

- Introducing a new topic
- Finding out what students know, or activating their prior knowledge

- Giving them a short, easy-to-read text about your topic

- Asking them to give you basic or beginner information about the topic

- Priming their brain for the next unit

- Introducing a new strategy to help them use later

- Asking them to define or explain vocabulary terms

- Reviewing or recalling what was already learned

- Identifying problems

- Sharing a website or explaining new technology

- Preassessing students before a unit or lesson

When you have one of these purposes for your target, you are most likely going to focus your questions and strategies within this zone. This zone promotes the other two by enticing the brain to further explore and own what is learned.

How to Build a Zone 1 Target

Remember that powerful targets have three pieces: (1) a verb for student thinking (Do), (2) specific content or skill students need to master (Know), and (3) a product to prove evidence of mastery (Show). Here is a list of Zone 1 verbs and verb phrases for your target to engage students in building basics:

- Explain what you learned in simple terms

- Define words that you learned

- Match ideas

- Recall rote learning (facts, lists)

- Draw a picture

- Share some basic information or processes

- Share what you know on a topic

- Respond with wonder and awe with a few of the facts

- Identify the following

- List

- Describe

- Answer

- Review

Your Do will be a simple-level verb from this list. Your Know will be simple facts or concepts from the chosen standard that students need to have engrained for success with the higher-level processing opportunities in Zone 2 and 3. Finally, it's time to decide on your Show, which is the product your students will create to prove they can think about the content at the required level, all while using the criteria for success.

Conclusion

By using Zone 1: Engage to Build Basics, you are sure to keep students engaged within the simple learning. Zone 1 focuses on developing background knowledge by pre-exposing students' brains to snippets of information before dumping the unit on them. It's a smart way to teach since all students will have neural networks established and ready to flourish and grow! In the next chapter, we'll explore ten strategies for Zone 1. We snuck in some higher-level thinking in these strategies too!

Getting Students to Care About Learning

- Tell them what's in it for them: "Who would like to learn a simple skill that can boost your achievement?"

- Share the target several times, visually too. Make sure they understand what is expected of them to learn that day. They can even chant it!

- Explain why the target is important to them currently and in the future.

- Help them connect that target to their life (activate their prior knowledge) and the world.

- Explain how this lesson connects to previous lessons and future lessons (common theme, essential question, and so on).

- Use their own experiences to validate an idea ("Have you noticed that . . .? ; Rate . . . ; What did you find in the text that said . . .?").

- Share what you learned ("I just read this new, amazing article . . .").

- Get them up and moving if they are hesitant at first. It's easier to listen and do when they are out of the chairs. Ask a little, and then take a lot of microsteps.

- Be enthusiastic about the lesson.

- Use the experimental strategy: "This is very new, so we'll see what happens."

- Plant powerful questions in their heads and get them wondering. Essential questions are great.

- Use framing, which is the ability to put an intentional bias on something to tilt their decision your way. The fire drill suddenly becomes "an unplanned energizer." The changes in schedule are "of great benefit because we finish up the unit sooner."

- Invite a student to start an activity or create an energizer.

- Engage students in stretching, energizers, and simple games such as Simon Says.

ASQ Time

1. **Action step:** What is the single most valuable next step you will take after having read this chapter?

2. **Summary of learning:** Summarize in three to five sentences what you learned in this chapter.

3. **Question:** What discussion questions do you have for other readers, for the authors, or for self-reflection to explore more from this chapter?

CHAPTER 5

STRATEGIES FOR ZONE 1

In the previous chapter, we explored how you can consciously prepare and prime your learners' brains and helped you discover what your learners already know (good, bad, right, or wrong). This step supports the process of making sense. Meaning-making becomes more powerful when we help students connect the new information to what they already know.

The CCSS ask us to plan more opportunities for students to speak, listen to one another, and write. Taking that directive into account, we've compiled ten strategies for building background knowledge and activating prior knowledge to help your students make more meaningful connections. While the other two zones have daily and long-term strategies, all strategies in Zone 1 are short and sweet. They can be done daily with any content and any target.

Building Background Knowledge Strategies

We have four great ways to build background knowledge in this engagement zone, including Pre-Exposure and Priming, *The Important Book*, the Historical Event Web, and Kinesthetic Vocabulary.

1. Pre-Exposure and Priming

Pre-exposure is a long-term advance notice. Just as studios and theaters want us to preview a movie to garner interest, pre-exposure is the process of covertly preparing students for future content or skills days, weeks, months, or even years before accountability. If you find yourself frustrated over the lack of background students have in a subject, you can build the background in class through pre-exposure. This process can be a bonanza for teachers who often get a blank stare from students when presenting new information. Pre-exposure is often based on skill acquisition (for instance, we prepare ourselves to eventually drive a car by driving a tractor, go-cart, or bumper car as a kid). We believe that "in a well-planned curriculum, students are getting pre-exposure all the time. For example, fourth graders can be exposed to algebra by working with symbols in basic problem solving, or they can prepare for geometry by building models that expose them to points, lines, planes, angles, solids, and volumes" (Jensen & Nickelsen, 2008, p. 74).

Priming is a short-term notice. It happens minutes or even seconds before exposure to a learning event. It prepares the learner for the understanding of concepts and gives the brain information to build into a semantic structure later on. It improves efficiency in the subject's ability to name a word, an object, and a concept or even perform a skill with some earlier exposure (Martin & van Turennout, 2002). In fact,

> Additional connections may have already been made to begin the more complex hierarchy. In either case, the systems and subsystems have turned out to be far more complex than earlier thought. The effects of priming may often be stored in such a way that they preserve data as well or better than if we purposefully learned it. (Jensen & Nickelsen, 2008, p. 75)

Preparation and Materials

Read through each of the activities in this strategy carefully to see what needs to be prepared beforehand. For instance, in Treasure Chest of Artifacts, you'll need to find and fill a cardboard treasure chest. For Book Tagging, on the other hand, you'll need to put together a collection of books that relate to your current unit. The key in these activities is to have your activities ready to go so that you can use them on a moment's notice.

Instructions

The following activities, all of which can be either pre-exposure or priming, should be used weeks or days before starting a big unit. They prepare the brain for the bigger chunk that units represent.

Treasure Chest of Artifacts

Find a cardboard treasure chest, and fill it with artifacts that go along with your unit (Jensen & Nickelsen, 2008). Ask students to add to the components of the treasure chest. During an ocean unit, for example, you can place books, shells, fossils, and plastic sea creatures in the treasure chest.

Book Tagging

Gather books about your unit. Allow students to choose a book to peruse. Students search for interesting quotes, pictures, captions, and graphs that they tag with a sticky note. On the sticky note, they should write why the element was interesting to them, documenting exact words from that page (Jensen & Nickelsen, 2008). These tags are then shared with other students. Our students like to sign the sticky notes to show ownership of the comment.

Ultimate Bulletin Board

Create an interactive bulletin board about your unit and post it about one week before the unit begins. Students are then able to catch the concept on the run. There are various ways to approach this bulletin board, including the following ideas: create a web of words that students will learn during the unit, type and post essential questions that will be part of the unit, ask students to write unit facts on index cards and post them, ask students to post pictures or graphics that support the unit, or recreate a word wall found on the Internet. Effective word walls are organized to show how the main term connects to other words or concepts. The central term should have a visual next to the word on the card. Print the cards so everyone can see the meanings from a distance and can play games and do activities with the words (in other words, use the words). Granite School District (www.graniteschools.org) has a great collection of CCSS math words for your word wall, separated by grade level. (Visit **go.solution-tree.com/commoncore** for a live link.)

Your Ticket In

Give students a sticky note before they leave your classroom. Tell them that in order to enter the classroom tomorrow, they will need to hand you this ticket with two or three of the prompts completed (Jensen & Nickelsen, 2008). You can choose certain ones or let them choose.

- What they know about the topic already

- An experience they've had with the topic

- A neat website that has information about the topic and what was learned from that website

- A drawing of what they think the topic looks like

- A question that they have about the topic

- Exact words from a text that goes along with the topic

IDEA Vocabulary Organizer

Preteaching vocabulary can improve comprehension (Laflamme, 1997). The National Reading Panel (2002) emphasizes that students benefit when they are taught the meanings of words before encountering them in the text and when they are provided consistent, ongoing opportunities to learn new words through reading.

Many wonder which words to preteach. Isabel Beck and colleagues created three tiers into which all words fall (Beck, McKeown, & Kucan, 2002). Tier 1 words are basic terms learned through conversation and daily experiences, such as *clock*, *sad*, and *baby*. Tier 2 words are general academic vocabulary that can be used in a cross-curricular manner in various disciplines, such as *considerate*, *altitude*, *industry*, *economy*, and *fortunate*. Tier 3 words are domain-specific words, such as *algebra*, *pronoun*, and *isthmus*. The CCSS encourage teachers to expose students to more Tier 2 words.

Teachers tend to do a great job teaching Tier 3, or domain-specific, words because they are relevant to the content at hand, such as *Newton's Third Law of Motion* (science), *onomatopoeia* (literature), or *polygon* (mathematics). While these words are great to know and are needed for the content area, educators often forget to expose students to the valuable, cross-curricular words of Tier 2, words they will encounter in all content areas. Tier 2 words are often precise, more fun ways of saying simple things, like *saunter* instead of *walk*. (Visit www.corestandards.org/assets/Appendix_A.pdf to understand all three tiers of words more fully. In addition, visit **go.solution-tree.com/commoncore** for live links found in this text.)

We like to use the IDEA Vocabulary Organizer (page 58) to introduce and elaborate on words our students will encounter during reading. Begin by using the Tier 2 word test to help you determine which words should be explicitly taught.

Tier 2 Word Test

1. Does this word allow students to express themselves in a more interesting and mature way than they otherwise might?

2. Is this word highly useful to students—in other words, can they use this word ten years from now?

3. Do students know related words that are simpler or less sophisticated so they can relate to this word and use it when needed?

4. Will this word help students understand the text?

Once you have chosen words, use this easy graphic organizer (figure 5.1) to build background knowledge before encountering the word within its context. You can actually use this method during instruction and afterward as well. It's the ongoing elaborative reviews that keep these words fresh in the mind so students can comprehend them, speak them, and write with them.

The first step is to create a table, as shown in figure 5.1.

WORD	I ILLUSTRATE (picture or symbol)	D DESCRIBE (pronunciation, part of speech, and description)	E ELABORATE (choose from elaboration list)	A ASSOCIATE (personal, meaningful sentence)

Figure 5.1: Sample blank IDEA Vocabulary Organizer.

Write the word in the first box, and include a sentence containing it from the text they are about to read. Next, fill in the *D* box. Define or describe the meaning of the word, the part of speech, and the pronunciation. Be sure to use student-friendly words in this description. It's also important that students can take your description and rephrase it with their own words. They can do this on the back of the IDEA form.

Now, photocopy the table for the students so they can fill in the rest. For *I*, or "Illustrate," students may draw a picture or symbol of the word or even search the Internet for an image to place in this box. Research shows that the nonlinguistic representation of the word is very important for students' memory and comprehension of a word (Marzano, Pickering, & Pollock, 2001). For *E*, or "Elaborate," encourage students to choose one of the following ways to go deeper.

- Basic elaboration ideas:
  - Give an example or non-example of the word.
  - Create clues about attributes of the word.
  - Give synonyms for the word.
  - Give antonyms for the word.
  - Explain how the word relates to your life.
  - Give additional information about the word (more facts).
- Challenging elaboration ideas:
  - Create a question about the word, then answer.
  - Create a simile, metaphor, or other figurative language using the word.

- Use the word in a different way from the original text.

- Create an analogy with the word.

- Paraphrase what the word means.

- Explain how the word relates to the world currently.

For *A*, or "Associate," have students include the word in a personal sentence; this makes it more relevant and, therefore, more memorable. See figure 5.2 for a completed organizer.

IDEA for Vocabulary Words

Unit: ___Government/Monarchy___ Date: ___October 13___

WORD	I ILLUSTRATE (picture or symbol)	D DESCRIBE (pronunciation, part of speech, and description)	E ELABORATE (choose from elaboration list)	A ASSOCIATE (personal, meaningful sentence)
Abdicate He abdicated his throne because of his announcement.		ab di kat Verb Give up power	Synonyms: Renounce Relinquish	I had to abdicate my iPod because of my bad report.
Dynasty The ruling dynasty must take a great deal of the blame.		di na stee Noun Powerful group that rules in succession	Synonyms: Royalty House	I don't think I'd want to be a part of a dynasty since I like to do my own thing. I wouldn't want to inherit my job.
Monarchy Charles II passed through Rochester on his way to London to restore the monarchy.		mon ar kee Noun Form of government in which one person is in control	Synonyms: Ruler Noble Example: King George	I'm glad we don't have a monarchy. I like our system of checks and balances.

Figure 5.2: IDEA Vocabulary Organizer for government and monarchy unit.

Source: Allen & Nickelsen, 2008. Used with permission.

To differentiate and give students a chance to process the words more deeply, you could also have them fill in all of the boxes. See page 76 for a reproducible version of the IDEA Vocabulary Organizer (Allen & Nickelsen, 2008). The IDEA Vocabulary Organizer is an ongoing document for review; it can also serve as a study guide before quizzes, tests, games, or products of learning.

Assessment

These pre-exposure and priming activities will prepare the brain for building more background knowledge. The brain loves to receive information in smaller chunks so it can properly digest this simple learning to build greater neural networks for complex thinking. When students have basic information in their brains, they will be successful when you later activate this knowledge.

2. The Important Book

In this strategy, students scrutinize the details of a topic's main idea. The first and second Reading anchor standards—"Read closely to determine what the text says explicitly and to make logical inferences from it; cite specific textual evidence when writing or speaking to support conclusions drawn from the text" (CCRA.R.1) and "Determine central ideas or themes of a text and analyze their development; summarize the key supporting details and ideas" (CCRA.R.2)—show that, as educators, we need to get students reading text closely in order to make logical inferences that support conclusions drawn from the text. Students should be able to determine the central ideas of a text and summarize the key supporting details and ideas.

The Important Book by Margaret Wise Brown (1949) will help students achieve both. This short picture book explains what is important about everyday things. This short, simple book has a pattern that helps students organize their learning into main idea and details. The first statement is the main idea throughout the book and then there are four to five details that relate to the simple everyday things. The most important idea is then rementioned at the end.

The Important Book Student Example

The important thing about cells is that they are the basic structure for all living things.

    1. Humans are made of over 100 trillion cells.

    2. Cells reproduce.

    3. Cells fight disease.

    4. The human body houses more bacteria cells than body cells.

    5. Cells contain the organism's DNA.

BUT the important thing about cells is that they are the basic structure for all living things.

Preparation and Materials

Share *The Important Book* with the class. You can use the reproducibles *The Important Book*: Primary (Grades K–3) and *The Important Book*: Intermediate (Grades 4–8) (pages 77–78 or online at **go.solution-tree.com /commoncore**) to show the template this book uses.

Instructions

Read *The Important Book* aloud. Next, after reading about your targeted topic, concept, or skill, have students complete a reproducible. They should evaluate what they think the author considers to be the most important aspect of the topic. Once they have determined what the author deems to be most important, they will choose three to five other important details (depending on the grade level) from the reading. Have them quote from the text to support how each detail supports the main idea.

Assessment

There are several ways to assess this strategy.

- Ask students to determine if the author's most important idea is congruent with what they think is the most important idea. Why, or why not?

- Have students provide evidence from the text that their chosen details support the main idea.

- Make sure all statements are accurate. Ask students to place a page number next to the facts.

For further extensions, try these ideas:

- Ask students to write an argument for or against what the author deems to be the most important aspect of the topic.

- Ask students to find more information on the topic on the Internet or in other media or texts to determine what another author deems to be the most important ideas. They would then compare and contrast these two perspectives.

- Ask students to evaluate the arguments and specific claims in the texts that they are using to determine the validity of the reasoning as well as the relevance and sufficiency of the evidence.

- Ask students to support all of their statements with details as to why those aspects are so important to the author. Add the word *because* after each statement.

- Because debates and argumentative writing will be important within the CCSS, *The Important Book* writing could be the beginnings of a minor debate about what students think are the most important aspects of an issue.

Students enjoy engaging in this background knowledge builder that introduces them to a topic with a quick writing activity. We celebrate these products by placing the final writing in the hallways. You could even ask students to use technology to produce and publish this writing.

3. Historical Event Web

The Historical Event Web (Jensen & Nickelsen, 2008) is a powerful tool to help students organize historical content while they are reading complex texts. The CCSS require students to write more nonfiction (CCR.W.2; CCR.W.3), and schools that have made nonfiction a top priority have had greater achievement than other schools (Reeves, 2003). This activity is the beginning of amazing nonfiction writing, but first we must build students' background knowledge on the nonfiction they will write. Many subject areas teach the history behind the events presented in the curriculum. For example, many technology classes study the history of computers, the Internet, and so on. Literature and art classes study historical events often too. Any class that teaches any type of historical event can use this web.

Preparation and Materials

Copy one of the Historical Event Web reproducibles based on grade level (pages 79–80 or visit **go.solution -tree.com/commoncore** to download). Prepare historical reading material that is interesting, complex, and based on your curriculum. Be prepared to support struggling readers during the reading of the complex text. See the CCSS's appendix B for strategies to support struggling readers with complex texts (NGA & CCSSO, n.d.a).

Instructions

Prep your students' brains before reading the historical content by doing a book or article walkthrough and looking at headers, changing some headers into questions, sharing a purpose for the reading, and activating their prior knowledge on this topic.

Have the students place the topic in the middle of the Historical Event Web graphic organizer (see figure 5.3) and brainstorm all of the facts and details about that event from the center to the outer sections. Students can come up with the who, what, where, when, why, and how of the event.

After you and the students have checked one another's historical webs for accuracy, students can determine how they are going to use this web to write a nonfiction piece. We know that brainstorming is one of the first steps to a good piece of writing. Brainstorms are often represented as a web. Writing anchor standard two asks students to "write informative/explanatory texts to examine and convey complex ideas and information clearly and accurately through the effective selection, organization, and analysis of content" (CCRA.W.2). To begin a piece of writing based on a brainstormed web, a student writes a thesis statement about the historical event. This thesis is the focus of the miniresearch he or she conducts. The student then lists main ideas and supporting details to support this claim and build the body of the writing. The student finally revisits the thesis with a strong conclusion.

Assessment

You may need to ask students where in the text they found some of the information they placed in the web. Encourage students to include page numbers by the facts just in case they need to give evidence later. Also have the students help you determine a rubric for expectations. You can search the Internet for other districts' rubrics for nonfiction writing.

Nonfiction writing is such a powerful tool for learning and ingraining information into our brains. Students can enjoy writing nonfiction when they have successfully built their background knowledge on the topic beforehand. These engaging graphic organizers can set students up for success with the writing process.

4. Kinesthetic Vocabulary

This vocabulary strategy helps students digest the most important description or explanation of a word's meaning so they can truly learn it for the long term and use it in their reading, writing, and speaking. This activity is a great example of the Common Core Speaking and Listening standards in action—kinesthetically, that is.

Preparation and Materials

Prepare and copy index cards with the definition or description of a word on one side and the word itself on the other side for about ten of the vocabulary terms students will encounter that week. The number of words

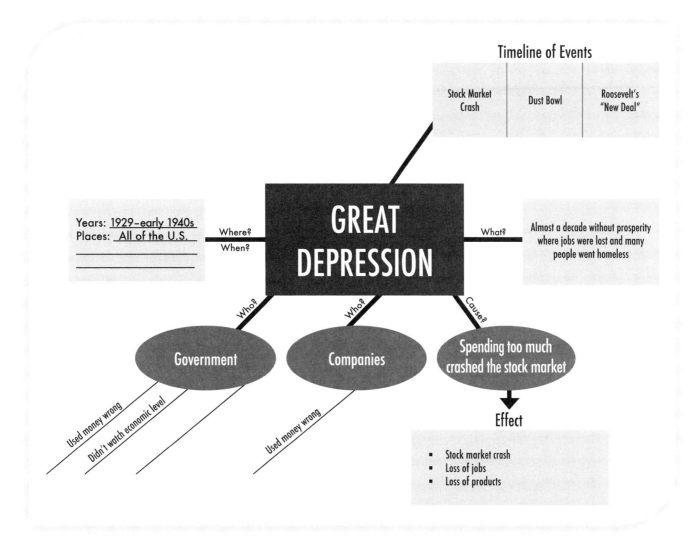

Figure 5.3: Historical Event Web example.

Source: Aubrey Nickelsen. Used with permission.

will depend on the age and intensity of the class, of course. Be sure to have the whole class pronounce each word correctly before playing the game.

Instructions

Place students in groups of four to five. Give them a stack of cards, or have them create the cards themselves on index cards. One student will act out a word; he or she should show the word side of the card to everyone in the group, say the word, and then act out the definition silently, like charades. The student keeps acting it out until someone in that group guesses the word's meaning. Students should have six to eight minutes for the entire game, taking turns acting out the words until someone guesses the definition. Once guessed, the actor or actress announces the definition written on the other side of the card. The next person then acts out his or her word. This continues until all definitions are acted out and guessed. Before the total time is up, students should review their definitions so that everyone remembers each word's meaning. The goal is for all students in that group to remember each definition after the allotted time.

Assessment

There are several ways to assess this strategy.

- Give a quick quiz the next day by providing the terms on a piece of paper and having students explain in their own words what each means. You will be ecstatic with how well they do on this quiz. Do tell them ahead of time.

- Go around to each group and ask them to choral yell the meanings of each word as you turn the card over. You will have enough time to look at their faces to see if they really know the words or not.

- Ask students to quiz each other in pairs and write on their door pass which words need more practice.

- Ask students to use a web diagram to show how the words are connected to one another. They can add other labels or concepts to help display the connections. Teaching vocabulary is teaching new labels for familiar concepts (Graves & Graves, 1994). Once an understanding of a concept occurs, then vocabulary can be connected to it. Vocabulary researchers believe that concept-based vocabulary instruction has the most lasting impact.

- Tired of matching vocabulary words as an assessment? Try Vocabulary Knowledge Proof. Students complete a table like that in figure 5.4 with the assessment vocabulary words. In the middle column, they rate their knowledge of the terms on a scale from 0 to 4:

  - 0 = I don't remember this vocabulary term at all.

  - 1 = I can draw a picture or symbol of this term.

  - 2 = I can draw a picture or symbol AND write the definition.

  - 3 = I can draw a picture or symbol, write the definition, AND give a real-world example.

  - 4 = I can do all of the above AND use the word in a different context.

- In the third column, they prove their rating by supplying knowledge of the term.

VOCABULARY TERM	LEVEL	PROVE IT
	0 1 2 3 4	

Figure 5.4: Vocabulary Knowledge Proof template.

To differentiate, try these techniques.

- If students struggle with these words, give more clues on the cards such as a visual or symbol.

- To challenge students, create a homogeneous group of students who need to be challenged and give them more difficult terms or concepts. You can also increase the ways they elaborate on the words in Vocabulary Knowledge Proof. Or ask them to engage in ongoing conversations using as many of the words as possible. They can keep track of the words used in the conversation by checking off the words as they speak them.

- You might need to stop the timer during the activity and ask students to do a quick review of the words they learned so far.
- For this activity to go smoothly, you might want the following roles in each group: timekeeper, material manager, encourager, and leader.

You will be surprised to see how well students remember these definitions. Then you can move on to exploring these words in greater depths.

Activating Prior Knowledge Strategies

We have compiled six great ways to activate prior knowledge within this engagement zone: Super Sleuth, Activating Prior Knowledge Dice, List-Sort-Label-Write, Carousel Brainstorm, Skimming and Scanning, and Reporter Goes Big Time.

5. Super Sleuth

Super Sleuth (Jensen & Nickelsen, 2008) activates prior knowledge before reading complex texts, writing, or experiencing explicit instruction. It can be used in any classroom with any content. This quick, engaging game gives students opportunities to engage with other students and the content by walking around the room, finding a peer, and asking that peer a question from their graphic organizer. We have yet to meet a student who doesn't want to engage in this activity.

Preparation and Materials

Fill in the boxes of the Super Sleuth reproducible (page 81 or visit **go.solution-tree.com/commoncore** to download) with questions you want students to discuss, then copy the page for each student. Each student also needs a pen or pencil. If using questions about vocabulary, read each vocabulary word aloud to the students so they know pronunciations.

Instructions

Give each student a copy of your Super Sleuth page. Have students approach each other, ask a question from one of the boxes, actively listen to the response, and then ask the other student to sign his or her name in that box. Then the student talks to another peer. This process continues until all questions have been answered or until the goal has been met.

The questions prompt discussion of what is already known about the topic (if priming strategies occurred, all students should have something to contribute). The goal is to get signatures, one per square, from different students while having rich discussions about what they are preparing to read, write, or learn. If you are pressed for time, ask students to get a certain number of signatures. If you have more time, ask the listening student to paraphrase what the peer said by writing responses in the box or on the back of the paper.

Assessment

There are several ways to assess this strategy.

- Ask students to answer the following questions on their door pass after a lesson introduced with Super Sleuth:
  - What was the most valuable piece of information that you learned during Super Sleuth?
  - What answer were you most proud of giving to another student?

- What question do you wish was on this Super Sleuth? We recommend telling the students about these three questions before they play the game so they are ready for them.

■ Walk around the room, listen to as many answers as possible, and document any neat comments, wrong information that you want to clarify, or even notes for the next time you do this activity.

■ Ask students to write additional information they learned from others on the back side of their Super Sleuth.

■ Hold a whole-group discussion about the most difficult questions.

In addition, there are many variations of Super Sleuth for your classroom.

■ **As a review of concepts learned:** You could fill the squares with tasks, such as "Find someone who can explain the differences between oceans and ponds."

■ **As an activating prior knowledge activity:** You could fill the squares with tasks, such as "Find someone who can tell you what percents and fractions have in common."

■ **As a preteaching tool for vocabulary:** You could place pictures in each box for your English learners to discuss. You can even insert descriptions and questions about the words (see figure 5.5).

■ **As a way to practice concepts:** You could fill the squares with tasks, such as "Find someone who can calculate: 23 × 46" or "Find someone who can create a complex sentence."

Super Sleuth		
Book: *Flipped* pp. 117–169		
Convolute (kon vo loot) V.: To roll one part over another; coil Have you ever been in a convoluted state? Explain.	**Imminent** (im e nent) Adj.: It is about to happen; especially about danger or catastrophe Can you think of an imminent event in someone's (friend or family) life?	**Askew** (E skyoo) Adj.: To one side; oblique-slanting Is there a position in life that you take on something that is askew?
Boycott (boi cot) V.: To refuse to use or buy Did you ever boycott anything in your life? Explain.	**Coaxing** (kōks ing) V.: To persuade with flattery and gentleness; bribery maybe Who do you need to coax, and why?	**Pungent** (pun jent) Adj.: Sharp to taste or smell; penetrating Describe a pungent smell that you have experienced recently.

Figure 5.5: Language arts Super Sleuth example.

Super Sleuths are one of our favorite ways to activate prior knowledge, since students are out of their chairs, focused on the curriculum, speaking and listening to one another, and preparing their memory systems for more content.

6. Activating Prior Knowledge Dice

This quick activity is sure to get students excited about the topic, but it also prepares them to write about that topic after learning more. Again, the CCSS have a strong message of more reading and writing in the classroom and less teacher lecture. Speaking and listening skills are enhanced with this small-group activity too.

Preparation and Materials

Divide students into groups of three or four. Distribute dice so each small group receives one. Display the following six questions and your topic so all students can see them (handout, SMART Board, and so on).

1. What are some facts that you know about this topic?

2. What are some synonyms (words that mean the same) for this topic?

3. What questions do you have about this topic?

4. Can you think of a specific time or example when you experienced this topic? If so, how did it affect you (benefits, cons, feelings, and so on)?

5. If you had time to draw a picture of this topic, what would you draw to represent this topic?

6. Why might it be important to learn about this topic?

Alternate questions include:

- Can you define this topic in your own words?

- What are other words that come to your mind when you think about this topic?

- What questions can you create about this topic for a future test or quiz?

Instructions

Have each student in a small group roll the die and think about how he or she will respond to the question represented by the number rolled. Since the questions are open ended, there should be a variety of answers for each question, but students are welcome to roll again if same numbers reoccur. The six questions should work with any content and activate the prior knowledge or experiences that students have regarding the topic. After each group has had their small discussion on the topic, a whole-class discussion about the topic can activate prior knowledge and build background knowledge.

Assessment

There are several ways to assess this activity:

- Walk around the room with your Cruisin' Clipboard (a clipboard with students' names written on forms so you can document mastery, comments, struggles, and so on), and write down any comments or misconceptions that will help you teach this lesson or unit better.

- Have students do a quick write on a half sheet of paper rating their background knowledge on the topic and why they gave themselves that rating.

- Have students list on their door pass what they want to learn more about after experiencing the lesson and the Activating Prior Knowledge Dice activity.

Activating Prior Knowledge Dice is a great way to kinesthetically get students communicating about what they know on the topic at hand. It only takes about four to six minutes depending on the group size that you use—very engaging!

7. List-Sort-Label-Write

This word-sorting strategy leads to powerful writing after the learning has been discussed in small groups. The CCSS ask us to use more cross-disciplinary Tier 2 words, which show up often while reading. It doesn't mean we can't teach the Tier 3 (domain-specific or subject-specific) words that are very specific and limited to our unit, but the focus should be on more Tier 2 words. We should keep this in mind while creating the words to use for this strategy.

Preparation and Materials

Divide students into groups of three to four. Cut ten to twenty index cards in half for each group to use as word cards. You'll also need sticky notes for labeling the category that the word cards are placed into and a book with a glossary or access to an online dictionary (www.ninjawords.com or www.merriam-webster.com) for searching definitions.

Instructions

The goal is for small groups of students to sort words or pictures that will be a part of the upcoming unit into like groups or similar chunks of information based on what they already know about the topic. Students should create categories that describe these groupings. Using sticky notes as category labels, students should group word cards around the most applicable category (see figure 5.6).

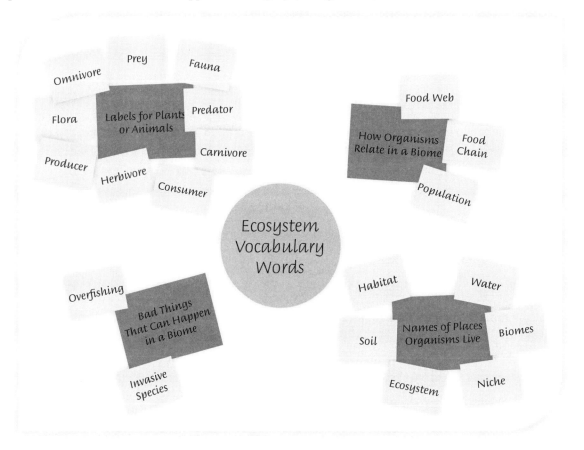

Figure 5.6: Example of List-Sort-Label-Write.

The discussion can be deep among the small group of students, and it helps build background knowledge among the students with a weaker schema on the subject. Use the following questions to help students converse within their group:

- Why does this word fit into this category?

- Could this word fit into other categories? Why, or why not?

- How do these two terms relate to one another? How has this web of words helped you understand the topic better?

- Can we add other words to this category?

The finished product for all groups will be a web of words placed within categories surrounding the main topic in the middle of the web.

After the learning, webs are powerful tools for writing research papers or reflections. You can have students show what they learned through writing paragraphs about the chunks of words they categorized. The writing could even be a group paper wherein each student writes about one of the categories.

Assessment

There are several ways you can assess this strategy.

- Ask students to take a photo of the before-learning web and after-learning web that they create. Then ask students to compare and contrast their learning in paragraph format.

- Ask students to self-assess and peer assess with the following criteria:

  - I contributed to sorting, defining words, and labeling categories.

  - I helped look up definitions.

  - I challenged the group with questions to rethink word and category placement.

  - I encouraged other group members to participate.

  - I performed the duties on my role card well because _____.

- Ask students to write about one of the categories they created and how the words connect with one another, or ask students to write a mini research paper on the big topic, but focus on two to three categories that they would like to learn more about. Create rubrics for expectations.

- Provide a door pass with the following questions:

  - From the List-Sort-Label-Write, I learned _____.

  - I have the following questions now: _____.

  - I could write a lot about the _____ category that we created.

This is a highly differentiated activity, since students place these cards into groups based on what they already know about the topic. You can make this a more challenging activity by not supplying the words and instead allowing the group of students to brainstorm ten to twenty words related to the topic and then sort them, adding about ten more challenging words that they need to sort, providing students with string or pipe cleaners to connect other words within other labels, and encouraging students to use resources such as books or the Internet to help them with their web.

You can simplify this activity by giving fewer words for the students to sort, providing the labels for the students (they still have to decide where to place the words), providing a glossary so students can look up the definitions of words, and helping them get started.

This kinesthetic sorting strategy provides higher-level engagement. Students enjoy this learning process much better than a worksheet full of words. Remember, it's not the final product that is important in this activity but rather the rich discussion that gets them there.

8. Carousel Brainstorm

This strategy gets students thinking quickly about open-ended questions on your current topic. It paves the path to better thinking, reading, writing, and discussions. Not only does it activate prior knowledge, but it also develops background knowledge if used appropriately.

Preparation and Materials

Create and present three open-ended questions that will activate students' prior knowledge on the chosen curriculum topic. An example of three open-ended questions for an American Revolution unit, for instance, might be:

- What motivates people to challenge a government?

- What problems might occur once a group challenges the government?

- How could the government respond to these challenges?

Give each student a sheet of letter-sized paper.

Instructions

The goal is for students to think about each question and write one to three different responses on their piece of paper. Ask students to get into groups of three and have each student write one of the questions in the center of his or her page with a circle around it. We recommend that you choose three higher-level, open-ended questions that really promote thinking about your topic. For example, "Why do you think it was called the Underground Railroad?"

Then, let the brainstorming begin. Have each student answer the open-ended question in the center of the page on a line extending from the center circle. When the answer is complete, the student passes the page to his or her left. This process repeats until each student answers each question by drawing a line from the center of the circle and writing his or her answer on that line. Because the questions are open ended, students might be able to answer the question more than once.

This activity takes about three to six minutes. Students then read each of the answers for all three questions. Share some aloud with the whole class.

Assessment

There are a couple options for assessing this strategy.

- Ask all the students who wrote down the first question to stand up and share the answers on their web. That way, you can all hear the answers and have discussions based on these answers. Do this for all three questions.

- Have students rate their overall answers for each question on a scale from 0 to 3:

- 0 = We didn't attempt to answer this question.
- 1 = We didn't know much about this question yet.
- 2 = We knew a few details but could learn so much more.
- 3 = We knew a lot of details and answered the question well.

These questions will bring about great discussion before the big lessons on the topic even begin. During this activity, students have the opportunity to jot some ideas and guesses down. They will be waiting to find out if they were correct—anticipation is a great emotion to elicit.

9. Skimming and Scanning

The CCSS ask all teachers to embrace the increase in reading nonfiction, and making connections with content area texts is imperative to successful nonfiction comprehension. Skimming and Scanning allows students to prepare their minds for a nonfiction text before reading it (Jensen & Nickelsen, 2008).

There is a myth out there that the CCSS prohibit teachers from setting purposes for reading or discussing prior knowledge (Shanahan, 2012). There was a time when the authors of the CCSS declared that there would be no before-reading strategies when reading complex text, but they had to delete this phrasing because of angry educators and researchers. In April 2012, the CCSS were revised to say that there is no ban on pre-reading strategies.

However, the CCSS still require that when reading complex text, students should gather most of the meaning by struggling their way through the first read. Rereading two or three times will occur when there is a close reading exercise with a complex text (see Zone 3 for close reading guidelines). Sometimes educators preteach too much before reading and assume that students with low background knowledge will be completely lost; the CCSS ask us to give students a chance to build some background knowledge with the first read rather than having us spoon-feed it to them. Skimming and Scanning is a helpful exercise because students find the answers to prep the brain rather than have teachers provide them. As Shanahan (2012) puts it, before-reading "preparation should be brief and should focus on providing students with the tools they need to make sense of the text on their own."

Preparation and Materials

Choose which Skimming and Scanning reproducible (pages 82–86 or visit **go.solution-tree.com /commoncore** to download) would be best for your students—primary (grades K–2), intermediate (grades 3–5), or challenging (grades 6–8)—and copy one per student.

Instructions

Students simply complete the reproducibles with the text on their own before reading. The reproducibles consist of a series of questions and book-analysis steps. Notice that the questions prime the students' brains for what the book might be about, but they also help the reader make some connections with content before the reading begins. This strategy preps the brain at just the right level without giving the reader too much information.

Assessment

There are various ways to assess this strategy.

- Walk around the room while students are completing the reproducibles, and stop to ask a few students questions about what they wrote.

- Have students share what they found with their peers.

- Discuss the purposes that they chose for the reading, compare them, and determine what the author might want the purpose to be.

- When questions come up, ask students which page or section of the text might have that answer.

Skimming and Scanning primes the brain and activates prior knowledge before reading occurs. It has a good balance of glossing the text without overdoing it. These questions can prepare the brain to be excited about the text as well, which improves the engagement level during the first reading of the text.

10. Reporter Goes Big Time

The purpose of this strategy is for students to become aware of what they know and don't know by conducting research on the curriculum topic and through question-and-answer conversations with one another (Jensen & Nickelsen, 2008). You can do this activity before learning a topic, during learning to check their thinking, or even after learning to prepare for a test. We are going to explain this activity as a pre-exposure activity. The Common Core Reading anchor standard seven ("Integrate and evaluate content presented in diverse media and formats, including visually and quantitatively, as well as in words" [CCRA.R.7]) and Writing anchor standard seven ("Conduct short as well as more sustained research projects based on focused questions, demonstrating understanding of the subject under investigation" [CCRA.W.7]) are supported by this strategy, since students will be integrating and evaluating content from diverse media and formats in order to complete this miniature research assignment. This activity helps students work with Speaking and Listening anchor standards one through three as well. (See page 28 for Speaking and Listening standards.)

Preparation and Materials

Pair students off, and copy one Reporter Goes Big Time reproducible per partnership (see page 87 or visit **go.solution-tree.com/commoncore** to download). For content background, you can use an article, book chapter, short nonfiction or fiction book, website article, and so on. Students will be reading this content and researching the points that your curriculum deems important.

It's more fun if you have students create, in advance, props for each of the two roles: reporter and expert. They won't know which role they're doing it for. While one half of the class gets reporter hats or name tags, the other half, the experts, will get some type of disguise (coat, rubber nose, glasses, and so on).

This activity works best when students brainstorm characteristics of good reporters and experts (how they act, facial expressions, and words they use). Remind them to keep these pointers in mind during the role play.

Instructions

Partner students to research the chosen curriculum topic. Make sure you think through how these partnerships will support one another during this learning process. Be very clear about what kind of information they are to seek out on this topic. You can give the partnerships:

- A list of concepts, labels, and phrases that are important so they can generate their own questions

- A list of questions that will be important during the unit (for those lower-background knowledge students)

- A checklist of items they are to research that helps them generate their questions (why an event took place, why a particular person was important during this event, how the events unfolded, cause-and-effect relationships, why the chemicals reacted the way they did, the steps in solving a word problem, why the author included these idioms, and so on)

The pairs first read to find the answers to the questions, stopping periodically to decide if the details in the reading really do provide answers. They then answer the questions about the content together and write the answers. This could take one day. We like to give our students a list of higher-level question stems to assist in the writing of these questions as well as many examples (see page 96 for examples of question stems to help you generate higher-level questions).

Assign or have the pair randomly draw one role card—expert or reporter—from a hat. Then take the partnerships and pair them with another partnership that picked the opposite role. In other words, two reporters are paired up with two experts. They keep what they drew out of the hat so that the number of reporters is equal to the number of expert pairs. It is at this point they don their costumes.

The reporters then take turns interviewing the experts using their set of questions, writing down the experts' answers so they can give them feedback after the role play. We like to use the Reporter Goes Big Time reproducible to keep this process organized and to check for understanding. Each expert answers the question asked of him or her but can get help from the other expert. The experts answer the best possible way that they know. They are allowed to look at their notes, their resources, or their prepared answers if that helps them.

Next, the two reporters switch roles and costumes with the two experts and use a new Reporter Goes Big Time reproducible to repeat the process. Once it is completed, give the foursome time to sit, debrief, and give each other feedback. Finally, students stand and share what happened and what they learned with the class.

Assessment

There are a couple ways to assess this strategy and use your assessment to help future lessons.

- Since this activity is a before-learning event, you will know concepts and ideas that still need more attention throughout the upcoming lessons or unit on this topic. Great preassessment data will help you drive your instruction and change your unit based on what you heard and saw. Walk around with your Cruisin' Clipboard and document misconceptions and amazing background knowledge.

- Study the Reporter Goes Big Time feedback column on the right-hand side. This will give you specific data to guide your unit.

To differentiate and simplify this strategy, give students only one text if they struggle with multiple texts. You could also give them a checklist to complete with the research requirements. To make the activity more challenging, don't support the students with any particular text but rather allow them to find one on their own with a visit to a computer lab or library.

This process of researching a topic and then asking students to role-play what they learned allows students to be creatively engaged in both the thinking process (question generation and answers) and the speaking and listening process. They will not forget this learning experience, and the researching, writing, and speaking and listening skills all support the CCSS.

Example of an Expert and Reporter Conversation on Darfur

Reporter: "Dr. Travelot, I heard that you just got back from Darfur. Where is it, and what's going on? Tell me what you saw."

Expert: "The armed conflict is in the Darfur region of western Sudan. It's mainly between the Janjaweed, a militia group, and farmers of the region. The Sudanese government has provided arms to support the Janjaweed and is targeting other ethnic groups. It's overwhelming. It rips your heart out. Children, lost, everywhere, and other children are recruited and have guns."

Reporter: "What is driving the conflict, and what can be done about it?"

Expert: "It's a combination of environmental mistakes and political corruption. Some call it a civil war, others, genocide. It's definitely worse than a civil war."

Reporter: "In your opinion, is this a problem, a serious problem, or an emergency and great international crisis?"

Expert: "Estimates of the number of deaths in the conflict have ranged from a low of 50,000 to as many as 450,000, and as many as 2.5 million are thought to have been displaced."

Reporter: "Could you share with our audience more about the people of Darfur?"

Expert: "There are many ethnicities and political or military groups. The Janjaweed is a militia group recruited from the tribes of camel-herding Arabs, and the farmers are the non-Baggara people as are the Fur, Zaghawa, and Masalit ethnic groups."

Reporter: "What are the locals saying has to be done?"

Expert: "It depends on who you ask . . ."

Source: Jensen & Nickelsen, 2008, p. 135.

Conclusion

Before getting into the higher engagement zones, it is essential to get the basics behind the learning. For a person to learn at higher levels, simple background knowledge should be in place. Every student comes to the learning journey with a different schema or background knowledge. Because of the vast differences among students, we need to use a variety of ways to activate prior knowledge so that new learning can become connected to each student's existing background knowledge.

The foundation has been laid after using strategies from Zone 1. Their brains have been primed by developing background knowledge with snippets of information. You have activated their prior knowledge in engaging ways. Now students should be ready to explore these topics further and in more depth. The next chapter explains how to help students engage to explore.

ASQ Time

1. **Action step:** What is the single most valuable next step you will take after having read this chapter?

2. **Summary of learning:** Summarize in three to five sentences what you learned in this chapter.

3. **Question:** What discussion questions do you have for other readers, for the authors, or for self-reflection to explore more from this chapter?

IDEA Vocabulary Organizer

Unit: _____   Date: _____

WORD	I ILLUSTRATE (picture or symbol)	D DESCRIBE (pronunciation, part of speech, and description)	E ELABORATE (choose from elaboration list)	A ASSOCIATE (personal, meaningful sentence)

Bringing the Common Core to Life in K–8 Classrooms ©2014 Solution Tree Press • solution-tree.com

Visit **go.solution-tree.com/commoncore** to download this page.

The Important Book: Primary (Grades K–3)

Text: _____

Author: _____

The most important thing about _____:

_____

_____

Write three other facts about _____:

1. _____

_____

2. _____

_____

3. _____

_____

The most important thing about _____:

_____

_____

_____

_____

The Important Book: Intermediate (Grades 4-8)

Text: _____

Author: _____

The most important thing about _____:

_____

_____

Write four to five pieces of evidence that the above is the most important thing (quote the text):

1. _____

_____

2. _____

_____

3. _____

_____

4. _____

_____

5. _____

_____

Most important thing about _____:

_____

_____

Do you agree or disagree with this author? Why?

Find another perspective on this topic and complete another *The Important Book* page. Compare and contrast the authors' views.

Historical Event Web: Primary (Grades K–3)

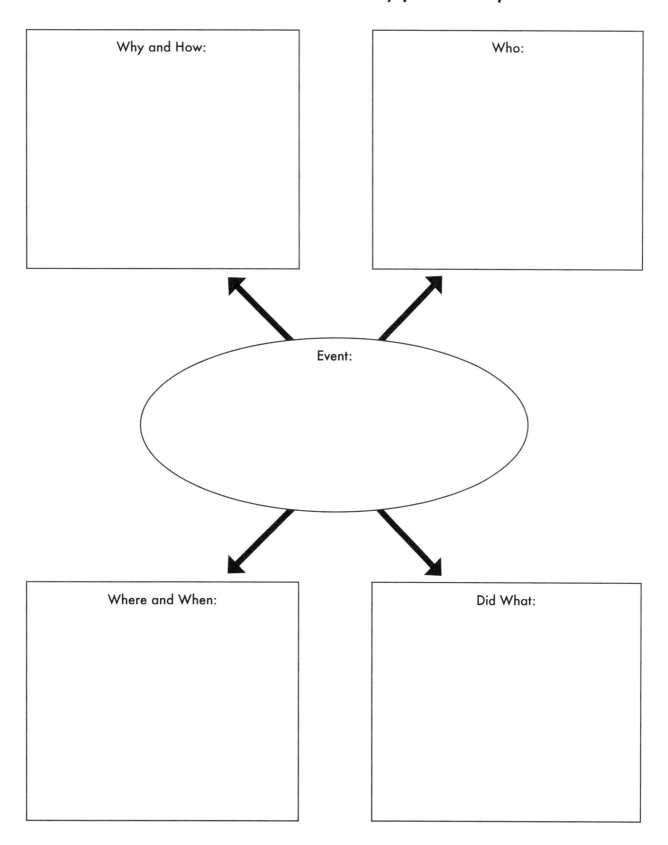

Why and How:

Who:

Event:

Where and When:

Did What:

Historical Event Web: Intermediate (Grades 4–8)

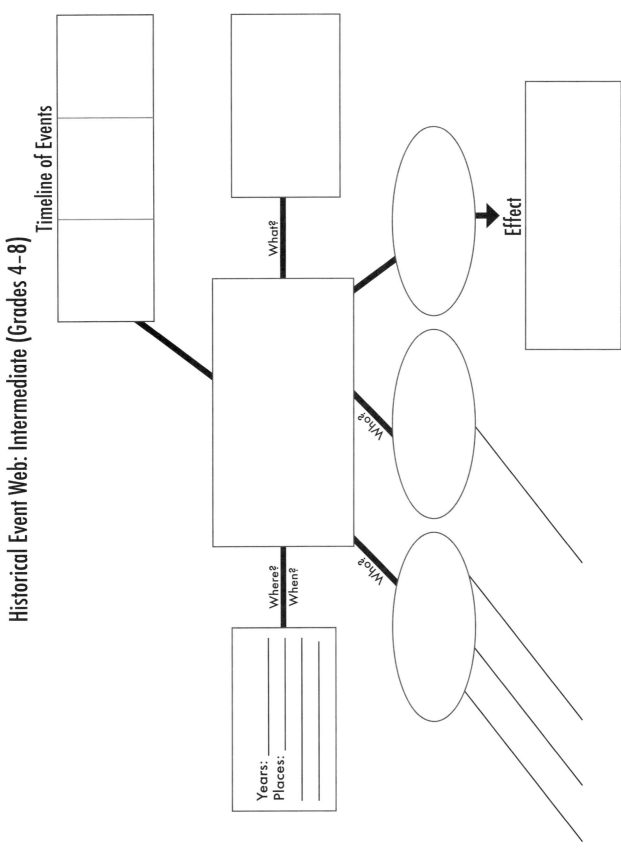

Timeline of Events

What?

Where?
When?

Who?

Who?

Effect

Years:
Places:

Jensen, E., & Nickelsen, L. (2008). Deeper learning: 7 powerful strategies for in-depth and longer-lasting learning. Thousand Oaks, CA: Corwin Press.

Super Sleuth

Name:		

Skimming and Scanning: Primary (Grades K–2)

Name: _____

Title of Book: _____

1. I pointed to and found the following within my book (check):

   ☐ Author   ☐ Boldface words

   ☐ Subtitles   ☐ Caption near pictures, diagrams, graphs, or charts

   ☐ Other: _____

2. What page is your favorite picture on, and why is this your favorite? Please describe. Page: _____

3. Write some questions that you would like answered about this book:

4. What do you know about this topic?

5. The purpose of reading this book is:

6. Let's define and draw pictures of the following words:

Word: _____	Word: _____	Word: _____

After-reading response:

Skimming and Scanning: Intermediate (Grades 3–5)

Name: _____

Title of Book: _____

1. I pointed to and found the following within my book (check):

☐ Table of contents   ☐ Boldface words that are defined in the glossary

☐ Index   ☐ Caption near pictures, diagrams, graphs, charts, and so on

☐ Titles and subtitles   ☐ Other: _____

2. What page is your favorite picture on, and why is this your favorite? Please describe. Page: _____

3. Write two different titles that you see within this book:

4. Write two different headers that you see within this book:

5. Write some questions that you would like answered about this book:

6. What do you know about this topic?

page 1 of 2

7. The purpose of reading this book is:

8. Let's define and draw pictures of the following words:

Word: _____	Word: _____	Word: _____
Word: _____	Word: _____	Word: _____

After-reading response:

Jensen, E., & Nickelsen, L. (2008). Deeper learning: 7 powerful strategies for in-depth and longer-lasting learning. *Thousand Oaks, CA: Corwin Press.*

Skimming and Scanning: Challenging (Grades 6–8)

Name: _____

Title of chapter or article: _____

1. Write the subtitles:

2. List the boldface words in this section of reading:

3. What page is your favorite picture on, and why is this your favorite? Please describe. Page: _____

4. List the titles of any graphs, data charts, diagrams, and so on that are within this reading section:

5. Write some questions that you would like answered about this reading:

6. What do you know about this topic?

7. The purpose of this reading is:

Reporter Goes Big Time

Directions: Complete this form for each question the experts answer. This page will be used to provide feedback to the experts on what they need to continue to learn. Your teacher wants to evaluate the answers too. When finished with the role play, staple this form to your list of questions asked this round.

Reporter: _____

Expert: _____

QUESTION (Reporter reads a question)	RESPONSE FROM EXPERT (Reporter writes a paraphrased answer from expert and name of expert)	EVALUATE EXPERT'S RESPONSE (Reporter checks the best option and explains where appropriate)
1		☐ Got it! ☐ Almost (explain): ☐ Not yet (explain): ☐ Needed assistance from other expert or notes
2		☐ Got it! ☐ Almost (explain): ☐ Not yet (explain): ☐ Needed assistance from other expert or notes
3		☐ Got it! ☐ Almost (explain): ☐ Not yet (explain): ☐ Needed assistance from other expert or notes

page 1 of 2

QUESTION (Reporter reads a question)	RESPONSE FROM EXPERT (Reporter writes a paraphrased answer from expert and name of expert)	EVALUATE EXPERT'S RESPONSE (Reporter checks the best option and explains where appropriate)
4		□ Got it! □ Almost (explain): □ Not yet (explain): □ Needed assistance from other expert or notes
5		□ Got it! □ Almost (explain): □ Not yet (explain): □ Needed assistance from other expert or notes
6		□ Got it! □ Almost (explain): □ Not yet (explain): □ Needed assistance from other expert or notes
7		□ Got it! □ Almost (explain): □ Not yet (explain): □ Needed assistance from other expert or notes

After this process, we now have the following questions for future learning opportunities:

CHAPTER 6

ZONE 2: ENGAGE TO EXPLORE

Have you ever poured vinegar on baking soda to create a volcanic eruption? Maybe you even mixed in red food coloring to make it more realistic. Science teachers can't wait to share this messy but fun experience with their students. When you watch the students, they are on their tippy toes waiting and wondering what will happen once the vinegar is poured onto the baking soda. Their curious faces are worth videotaping and saving for a lifetime. They wonder how on earth those two ingredients cause the fizzing, mini-eruption coming out of the fake volcano; thus Zone 2 learning starts.

Once students are oriented, the next step is to invite them to explore the content at higher levels of thinking. A key cognitive strategy that well-prepared college students use is researching content deeply to answer questions they have (Conley, 2010). Exploring appropriate, credible, and varied resources is part of this process. During Zone 2: Engage to Explore, we want students grappling with questions about the content. This zone helps students wonder about, connect with, and imagine the content. It's the spark for wanting to learn more. It is the impetus toward a love of learning. Without this zone, content can become meaningless, boring, and irrelevant. Key words that define this zone are: *questioning*, *connecting*, and *curiosity*.

Asking Questions to Keep Students Engaged

The key to getting students thinking at levels they don't even realize they're capable of is to ask questions and be curious about the content. As educators, our role is to ensure that our students have the background knowledge to be successful when answering these questions. Asking compelling questions not only raises engagement but also contributes to student achievement with a significant 0.47 effect size (Hattie, 2009). In addition, fostering questions helps promote students' cognitive development (Chouinard, 2007).

Expect all students in your classes to respond in some way. In more traditional classrooms, students who don't raise their hand know that the students who always participate will answer for them. When we allow this, we are robbing the less-engaged students of an opportunity to strengthen their brain. Ask questions that reflect your target, and ask all students to respond, whether on sticky notes; to their partner verbally; on a gel, chalk, or dry-erase board; or in a journal. Be sure to give students some way to respond, even if it's as simple as, "I don't know, but I'd like to know." Strong questions will help students stay engaged at higher levels. Another benefit is that fewer behavior problems occur, since students know they are held accountable for what is being taught.

We can use strategies, activities, assessments, and questions to take the brain into the Engage to Explore zone. Some questions and question stems that might help you plan for this zone include:

- Does this information remind you of anything from your personal life? Objects? Events? Person? Process?

- How does this information connect with other things you have learned (books, stories, websites, current events, and famous people)?

- How would you explain this information to someone four years younger or four years older?

- How could you implement what you learned in the future (career), in your household, at school, in the community, or in the world?

- What simile, metaphor, or analogy could be created based on what you learned?

- What if _____?

- What do you think _____ would have done if _____?

- What else could _____ have done?

- How does this information connect with _____?

- What do I think of when I hear _____?

- Why is this relevant to me?

- What examples would support this content?

- How would you organize _____ to show _____?

- What would you compare _____ to or with?

- What does _____ have in common with _____?

- How is _____ different from _____?

- How might you go about researching this topic or question?

- What subtopics need to be studied in order to understand this big question or topic?

Now that you have some powerful question stems that can be placed strategically within your daily lesson plan, it's time to decide when to use strategies from this zone and how to build the best target.

When to Use Zone 2

After students have ample simple learning opportunities in Zone 1, it's time to take them through Zone 2, although many students can jump to this zone on their own. All lessons should begin with a hook to gain buy-in. Be sure to answer the "What's in it for me?" question in each student's mind. Sometimes in Zone 1, students remember the facts and content as unrelated, unconnected lists of facts, and we all know that unconnected facts don't last. It's interconnected content that makes for longer-lasting, deeper learning. In this zone, we explain to our students why the target for today's lesson is important to them now and in the future. Thus, in Zone 2, we prepare them for the relevance.

You'll want to generate a lesson within this zone when you have one of the following purposes in mind for your lesson:

- Encouraging students to generate questions on the topic

- Wanting students to get creative with content, to imagine, to wonder

- Connecting existing background knowledge with new knowledge

- Asking students to compare and contrast information

- Incorporating more meaning with the content; connecting it with the students' personal experiences or knowledge

- Wanting students to research the topic in more depth by using credible, appropriate resources to find answers to research questions

- Desiring students to get excited and want to learn more about the content or skill

When you have one of these purposes for your target, then you are going to need strategies from Zone 2: Engage to Explore. It's time for students to put on the explorer's hat and wonder. They can only do this if they believe they can take risks in your classroom. Again, a positive learning culture is the foundation of a highly engaged classroom.

How to Build a Zone 2 Target

Remember that powerful targets have three pieces: (1) a verb for student thinking (Do), (2) specific content or skill students need to master (Know), and (3) a product to prove evidence of mastery (Show). Here is a list of Zone 2 verbs and verb phrases you could use in your target to engage students:

- Generate questions

- Compare and contrast information with something you already know or have experienced

- Sort words or objects into similar categories based on what you know

- Make connections with content and among other disciplines

- Make content relevant to your personal life

- Create analogies, similes, and metaphors for the learning

- Visualize how to apply the information in the real world and to specific situations

- Discover

- Solve

- Experiment in order to find out

- Build _____ in order to determine

- Dissect

- Infer

- Survey

- Research

These are just a few of the verb phrases that might appear within your target. Do you see how these verbs force the brain to think at higher levels? The second part of a powerful target is the specific content, the Know, pulled from the standards. You will refer to your standards and curriculum for these details. Finally, it's time to name how the students will show you that they can think about your content at the required level—using the criteria for success to create their product. Some of the products could be the resources for strategies within this zone.

Conclusion

This chapter explains Zone 2: Engage to Explore by setting the stage for exploring content through asking questions and researching. Remember, the CCSS want us to engage students with short and longer researching opportunities. The next chapter will focus on the many strategies available to implement this zone in your classroom.

ASQ Time

1. **Action step:** What is the single most valuable next step you will take after having read this chapter?

2. **Summary of learning:** Summarize in three to five sentences what you learned in this chapter.

3. **Question:** What discussion questions do you have for other readers, for the authors, or for self-reflection to explore more from this chapter?

CHAPTER 7

STRATEGIES FOR ZONE 2

This chapter covers both in-depth research strategies that take students deep into the content and daily exploration strategies that, though quick, still challenge students. Both sets of strategies keep the brain focused on exploring content at deeper levels using questions.

In-Depth Research Strategies

We begin our list of Zone 2 strategies with the Big 6 Research Process. The Big 6 is so powerful that we decided to give additional ideas to support this excellent research process. Thus, the other strategies in this section—Produce, Improve, Prioritize; Brainstorming Bonanza; Finding Credible and Accurate Resources; and Speak What You Know—support this process in more detail. This higher-level thinking process will challenge and engage students in each step.

11. The Big 6 Research Process

The CCSS Writing anchor standards ask students to use focused questions to demonstrate understanding of the subject under investigation. Students will also need to gather relevant information from multiple print and digital sources, assess the credibility and accuracy of each source, and integrate the information—all while avoiding plagiarism. This writing process could possibly take your students through nine of the CCSS Writing anchor standards (not number three, since it won't be a narrative).

Our students have been very successful with a research method that Mike Eisenberg and Robert Berkowitz (1999) founded—the Big 6. It's a six-step model to help anyone solve problems, complete research, or make decisions by using information learned.

Preparation and Materials

Choose topics that students will research within your curriculum (social studies, science, famous mathematician, author, time period, and so on). Prepare the resources that your students will pull the information from. Find safe websites that they are able to use, library books on the topic, and helpful articles. You can have them find these resources themselves too.

This is a long-term research project that could take students a week or two to complete depending on your requirements and how much time they have daily to work on the project in your classroom and at home.

Set due dates for each question or a set of questions (you know your students best and how often they need conferences and checkpoints). You could differentiate this process as well: check in more often with students who need frequent feedback. No matter what, never check a student's work at the end—there won't be enough time for him or her to change what is needed. The goals are learning the content, explaining it in writing, using the research process, and sharing what is learned. Your job is to help them accomplish these goals!

Determine if you will partner students for this research project or have them do it individually, or a little bit of both depending on student needs. We recommend that partnerships or individuals have different topics (connected with your curriculum, of course) so peer learning can occur, and there won't be competition for limited resources.

Create a reminder poster with the Big 6 steps (you can also search for such a poster online):

1. What is the problem?

2. What sources should you use to answer this question?

3. Where are the best resources located?

4. How will you document what you are learning?

5. How can you best organize and synthesize all the information?

6. Did you solve your problem or answer your question? How will you evaluate whether or not you reached your goal?

A rubric of expectations for each step should be given to the students before they start this process in order to make sure they understand each requirement. This rubric or checklist will be designed based on your grade level, your topic, the skills you have already taught them, your school or district writing expectations, and so on. Take the time to do this piece well—it sets the stage for how students will evaluate their success along the journey. It will guide how you differentiate for different students in your classroom.

Instructions

Have students go through the steps and respond to each question with the topic in mind. This will take some time, many resources, and a schedule to complete this long-term research project. You can create a graphic organizer for each step to keep them organized or find one online.

For step one students should create a question that they want answered about your topic, define a problem that they want to find solutions to, or define the task at hand. To get students started with step one, write the problem—which should be narrow and clear—as a question that the students want to answer with research. Some examples of research questions: How did the Underground Railroad work to save so many slaves? Do you think our world will run out of valuable natural resources (pure spring water, oil, fossil fuels, and so on)? Why does the Pythagorean Theorem work? Guide your students in learning to ask more essential questions. For additional lists of questions and more information about creating essential questions, see *Essential Questions* by Jay McTighe and Grant Wiggins (2013).

For step two, students should seek resources that are available to them in the school library, public library if they have access to it, online, through people to interview, and so on. Students should choose their top three resources. They can refer to almanacs, websites, biographies, family members, community members, YouTube, experts, nonfiction books, newspapers, and so on.

For step three, students should determine where the information is within each source (such as chapters, pages, paragraphs, or webpages). They can use the resource tracker on page 113 to evaluate the accuracy and credibility of the sources they choose. In this step, students prioritize their resources.

During step four, have students determine if a notebook, note cards, NoodleTools (www.noodletools .com), recording device, mindmap, or some other tool will be the designated way to collect the information. Students should create a system for citing the sources as well. They will be reading, viewing, or listening to their resources and documenting what they are learning so they can use this information for the final products.

In step five, students need to decide how they will share the learning—by presenting it, making a PowerPoint, creating a mindmap of it, creating an interview about it, and so on. This will help them determine how they will organize all the information they just collected. Have students consider what product will help them best share what was learned. They will be taking the information from step four and synthesizing it into a product that brings the pieces together.

Step six is the stage at which students ask, "Did I solve my problem or answer my question? How could I have done a better job? How could I improve my research process the next time?"

Assessment

Students should self-evaluate throughout this research process, and you should have check-in points with due dates along the way rather than one big due date.

We recommend a rubric that includes all of the steps. List everything you expect to see and hear at each step so that students know exactly what you want. You can search online for "Big 6 research method rubrics" to find several options, or you can create your own based on your grade-level needs.

Be sure to give students feedback along the way so they can correct mistakes and ensure the information they are gathering is really answering the big question. Check-in points will help ensure they understand the research process and are doing it accurately.

12. Produce, Improve, Prioritize

The Common Core Writing anchor standard seven asks students to "conduct short as well as more sustained research projects based on focused questions, demonstrating understanding of the subject under investigation" (CCRA.W.7). How can we get our students to create focus questions that will lead them on a journey of fabulous research? The following steps will help students create the best research questions. This one activity will help them with the Big 6 Research Process step one of defining the problem or creating a question.

Preparation and Materials

Create a poster of the three steps—(1) produce your own questions, (2) improve your questions, and (3) prioritize your questions—so the students are reminded of them throughout the school year. Choose a topic from your standards and provide blank paper to students you've organized into small groups. Bring a unique or humorous photo from your life to class.

Instructions

Show the students your photo, but don't explain it. Tell the students you are going to play a game with them called Good, Better, Best. They are to create a good, lower-level question about the photo—a question that has a one-word answer. Have students ask these questions to you as a whole group. Answer their lower-level questions. If they ask a higher-level question during this time, tell them to save it for the next round. Next, students create and ask a higher-level question. Refer to Zone 2 question stems on page 90 for ideas to share with them or Question Stems to Help You Generate Higher-Level Questions (page 96).

Question Stems to Help You Generate Higher-Level Questions

What questions do you have about _____?

How would you summarize _____?

If you could include one more chunk of information, what would it be?

What did you rediscover about _____?

Do you have any personal connections with _____?

How would you explain _____ to _____?

How could you implement the information about _____?

How will your life be different now that you have learned _____?

What analogy or simile can you create after learning about _____?

What are your gaps in thinking on _____?

What are you beginning to wonder now that you have learned _____?

What was the main idea of _____?

What are some cause-and-effect relationships that you saw in the section about _____?

What was the most important information that you learned about _____?

How would you organize _____?

What would happen if _____? What would happen next?

How can you design, invent, compose, or arrange _____?

Can you propose alternative solutions and arrangements for _____?

How would you modify _____?

What could be done to minimize/maximize _____?

Can you formulate a theory for _____?

Do you agree or disagree with _____?

How do you feel about _____ and why?

Which is better, and which is worse?

Which solution is best, and why?

How would you sort and label these groups of words?

How does _____ compare/contrast with _____?

What are the pros/cons for/against _____?

What might the next section be about, and why did you say that?

What was the purpose of this section/paragraph/sentence? Give evidence from text.

How could you compare and contrast _____ with _____?

Why is/did _____? Give evidence from text.

Can you explain _____ in more depth?

Where else was that said? Where else could _____? Why?

What is the effect of _____ on _____? Give evidence from text.

Why did the author believe/say/write _____?

What was the MVPI (Most Valuable Piece of Information) and why? Give evidence from text.

If you could change _____, what or how would you do it? Why?

Ideally, a student's first question is good and the second question is better. Guide students by asking, "Are you sure that is a better question? How do you know?" These better questions should be more open ended but shouldn't require you to think as much as the next level (best).

Finally, for the grand finale, have students create and ask the best, highest-level questions about the photo. Congratulate them on generating their own questions. Your students will understand the photo so much better after they go through all question types: good, better, best.

Tell them there is a three-step process they can go through to brainstorm the best research questions (adapted from Rothstein & Santana, 2011). The stronger their background knowledge on a topic, the better the questions can be (they should have been learning about the topic somewhat before doing this activity if it is leading them to a research project). Sometimes we use this three-step process just to generate great questions before closely reading text. Questions are powerful and help the students stick with a challenging text rather than abandoning it.

1. Produce your own questions:

    •   Ask as many questions as you can.

    •   Don't stop to discuss, judge, or answer the questions.

    •   Write down everything exactly as it is stated.

    •   Change any statement into a question.

2. Improve your questions:

    • Categorize them as closed or open ended.

3. Prioritize your questions:

    • Choose the three most important open-ended questions and explain why they are top priority.

Now students are ready to start a research project in small groups to explore the answers to these stellar questions or they can start reading about the topic with the purpose of finding the answers to the questions.

Assessment

Have students do a group assessment after completing the three-step process. See figure 7.1 for a sample assessment.

Students will be highly engaged in this small-group activity, which teaches one of the most important comprehension strategies out there: students generating their own questions. This three-step strategy can be used across the disciplines, with research, during and after reading, and even while explicit instruction occurs.

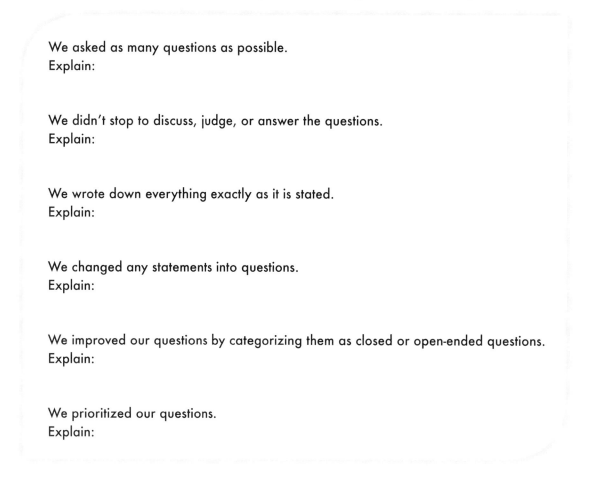

We asked as many questions as possible.
Explain:

We didn't stop to discuss, judge, or answer the questions.
Explain:

We wrote down everything exactly as it is stated.
Explain:

We changed any statements into questions.
Explain:

We improved our questions by categorizing them as closed or open-ended questions.
Explain:

We prioritized our questions.
Explain:

Figure 7.1: Sample group assessment for Produce, Improve, Prioritize.

13. Brainstorming Bonanza

This strategy is a great next step in the Big 6. It will help students determine which aspects of the topic they want to dive more deeply into. Students will find perspectives and content on their topic by gathering research.

The goal is to get new content and different perspectives from three to eight (depending on grade level and student readiness levels) books, authors, websites, experts, media, news magazines, or journals on the topic.

Preparation and Materials

You'll need library access for books, computers with Internet access, magazines, and journals. Copy the Brainstorming Bonanza (page 111 or visit **go.solution-tree.com/commoncore** to download) for each student.

Instructions

The first key is to hook students' attention. This can be accomplished in many ways—by providing a good story, a personal experience of yours, a cliffhanger, or personal connections with your students (consider what is part of their world).

Model the three steps of the Brainstorming Bonanza process before having students do it independently. After you've shown them how, have students complete the Brainstorming Bonanza reproducible in steps. If necessary, you can pair students up until they feel comfortable using this process independently.

In step one, have students brainstorm resources they could use to learn more about their topic. The graphic organizer groups resources as follows: Internet resources; books, journals, and newspapers; and other people (see figure 7.2, page 100). Students should go to the library, get on computers, and even make some phone calls or send texts, tweets, or Facebook comments to determine the expert resources that could be used for their topic. They then list these resources in the appropriate boxes for step one.

In step two, students look through their resources and list subtopics of the larger topic. In other words, we want students to take a broad category like "tornadoes" and break it down into several subtopics such as: worst ones, damage, safety precautions, weather conditions, deaths, injuries, history, and so on. They find these subtopics in their resources and organize around the main topic, with spokes of words fanning out from the center.

Finally, in step three, students determine which of these subtopics will be explored in the future research project or writing by circling the subtopics that most interest them.

Assessment

Give students this minichecklist to determine if they are on the right track with this important step to the research process:

- I have at least three different sources from each category that I can use for brainstorming subtopics.
- I did some preliminary research to determine my subtopics that are within the web.
- I believe my subtopics are appropriate and accurate for this larger topic.
- I narrowed down which subtopics I will include in my future research.

See page 112 or visit **go.solution-tree.com/commoncore** for a reproducible version of this checklist.

With these resources, students will discover that far more is out there than they originally thought. Ultimately, students will develop a wider, more professional landscape of subtopics that better prepares them for writing and presenting their new learning of the topic.

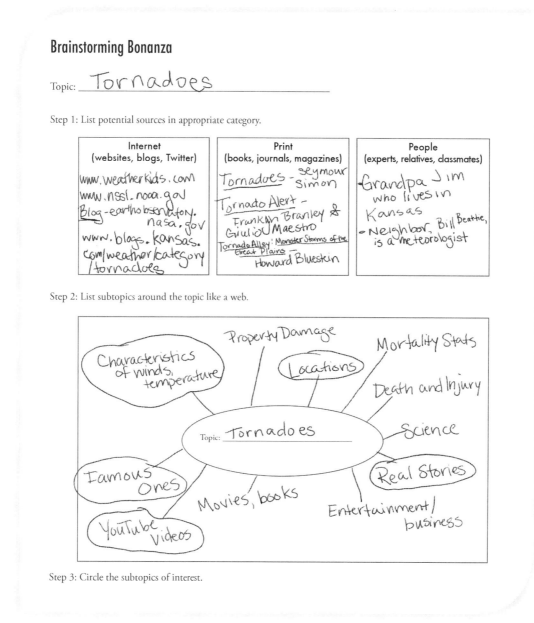

Figure 7.2: Example of Brainstorming Bonanza.

14. Finding Credible and Accurate Resources

The Common Core Writing anchor standard eight asks students to "gather relevant information from multiple print and digital sources, assess the credibility and accuracy of each source, and integrate the information while avoiding plagiarism" (CCRA.W.8). Students then need to take this credible and accurate information and use it to support their analysis, reflection, and research on the topic at hand. This thinking process is supported by an easy-to-use graphic organizer.

Preparation and Materials

We recommend starting the evaluation process of a resource with the reproducible Credible and Accurate Resource Tracker (page 113 or visit **go.solution-tree.com/commoncore** to download). After determining which sources are most credible and accurate, students will dive deeply into reading those resources to get the gist of the author's perspectives. They can then use the Different Perspectives reproducible (page 114 or visit **go.solution-tree.com/commoncore** to download) to document their thought process on the different perspectives. This final thinking process could possibly even make the researcher change his or her mind regarding whether or not the author is accurate and credible. The Different Perspectives reproducible supports Reading anchor standard nine—"Analyze how two or more texts address similar topics" (CCR.R.1).

Note that the Different Perspectives reproducible is not necessary; it is just the next step to determine if the source is reliable.

Instructions

Start the lesson with these questions for the students: What kinds of sources should you use? What is critical to know about your resources before using them in your research, writing, or projects? Students should understand that sources need to be reliable, credible, trusted, accurate, unbiased, balanced, and so on.

Next, teach the following pointers for evaluating the credibility of a resource (give them examples of each):

- Compare multiple sources as a search strategy to see if there are consistencies among the sources to prove credibility.

- Determine if the writing seems too good to be true. Does the information seem believable? Does it make sense? Is the information exaggerated in any form? How can you check to determine if it is true?

- Determine if the author is credible, popular, or an expert on the topic. Who is the author (education, training, experiences, professional title or degree, other books)? Is the author connected to respected, professional organizations?

- Determine if the information is current. Is there a date for the information written? What are the dates on the websites, books, resources that he or she quotes, and so on?

- Check the works cited or bibliography of the source to determine if the information presented has substantial research to support it.

- Evaluate the source's style, tone, and details. Are there grammar, spelling, punctuation, or capitalization errors? Is the writing emotional, bitter, critical, or demanding? Is the tone extremely biased and one-sided? Stay away from biased information that manipulates people.

Have students use this information to complete the graphic organizer, the Credible and Accurate Resource Tracker reproducible or the Different Perspectives reproducible, and conclude which resources or perspectives are credible and why. Once this happens, students can start to use the sources for research.

Assessment

There are several ways to assess this strategy.

- Have peers ask one another which resource was the least credible and accurate and why. Then have a whole-class discussion asking students which of the pointers for evaluating the credibility of a resource played a role in their decision.

- Take your Cruisin' Clipboard, with student names on a form to check for understanding and mastery, and walk around to students to check how they are completing the reproducible. Ask them some questions as well, such as: Why did you respond that way? How did you find that resource? What did that resource have to say about . . . ?

- Have students explain which resources they will be using in their research project and why they chose those resources.

This strategy is a challenging one but is a must for the anchor standards focused on research. Students are quite engaged during these activities, since they want to prove how credible or accurate a resource is. They just need to be prepared to explain why.

15. Speak What You Know

The CCSS expect students to have numerous opportunities to present what they are learning. The standards require that students gain, evaluate, and present increasingly complex information, ideas, and evidence through speaking and listening as well as through media. All six of the Speaking and Listening anchor standards can be reached through this activity depending on your specific requirements.

Preparation and Materials

Adjust the presentation rubric to meet the needs of your students (see pages 115–117 for reproducible versions of the rubric for various grade levels or visit **go.solution-tree.com/commoncore** to download). Print a rubric for each student ahead of time so the students know exactly what is expected and how to prepare accordingly. Make sure students can explain what each criterion in the rubric could look and sound like during a presentation.

The Presentation Rubric: Primary (Grades K–3) reproducible was created as a student self-assessment rather than teacher evaluation tool. We recommend asking the student what he or she thought about the presentation and then share what you wrote down for each rubric area during the presentation. Remember, this is not graded; we are just trying to help them on the journey of public speaking. Make sure to give verbal feedback on how the student marked his or her rubric.

The Presentation Rubric: Intermediate (Grades 4–8) reproducible was created for a teacher or peer to complete during the presentation (Jensen & Nickelsen, 2008). We like to give two to three of these out to other students while we are also evaluating the speaker. This form could easily be turned into a student self-assessment form as well.

If you don't want to give out the form to students, you could have about three students do a peer review by using the following steps: praise (give two positives about the presentation); question (note any questions about the content); and polish (note what the student could improve on next time).

The bottom line is that the more feedback students receive from a variety of people, the more improvement can be made the next time.

Instructions

Deliver a minipresentation that exaggerates the rubric criteria. Here is an opportunity to be very dramatic, funny, and creative. Act out a part of your life and use gestures to explain just how big that fish was that you caught or just how long your hair was in the 70s. The focus is not on the content but on your delivery of the content.

Give each student a copy of the rubric, and while you are presenting, tell them to check off each criterion when they see or hear it. After the presentation, have them give you feedback on what they liked and what could be improved. When they do this, refer them to the rubric criteria to make connections. Categorize the list of items they mentioned in the presentation. You can do this with a T-chart labeled "Sounded Like" and "Looked Like." Some items, like gestures, eye contact, and facial expressions, will not have an auditory example. Vocal variety, on the other hand, will not have a visual example. For example, when students brainstormed what "organization" sounded like, they said teachers used transition words such as *first*, *second*, then *finally*.

Explain to the students what they really need to implement in their upcoming presentation. Give them opportunities to practice their presentation while emphasizing each criterion on the rubric.

Assessment

There are a couple ways to assess this strategy.

- See the Presentation Rubric: Primary (Grades K–3) reproducible. Teacher and students will use this tool.

- See the Presentation Rubric: Intermediate (Grades 4–8) reproducible. Teacher and students will use this tool.

To differentiate for simplicity when first using the rubric or for students not used to presentations, ask students to cross off one section of the rubric that they don't want to be evaluated yet, such as gestures or eye contact.

To challenge students, ask them to take one criterion and add more detailed expectations to that area. For example, if the student wants to sound like an expert with his or her content, the criterion should be to cite at least three to four experts during the presentation or to use professional visuals to explain content.

Presenting can be a very stressful event for many students, but the more they are exposed to talking with their peers in small ways such as cooperative learning, think-pair-share, or games, the easier presentations will become. Help students view speaking opportunities as a time to teach their peers—to help them grow as learners. Speaking is a highly engaging activity in that it involves the affective, behavioral, and cognitive components of engagement. Students are emotional when they are in front of their peers in the spotlight. During their presentation, they are totally focused on the task at hand, and their brains are active as they synthesize what they learned to share with others.

Daily Exploration Strategies

The strategies in this section—Quad Cards, Reflective Conversations, H Diagram, and Stump the Chump—can be implemented within a daily lesson plan and still challenge the brain to think at higher levels. Students will love these Engage to Explore strategies, which are short and sweet compared to the longer research strategies listed previously.

16. Quad Cards

How can you help students develop more in-depth understanding and meaning? One of the best strategies to improve comprehension is inviting students to generate questions during and after reading (Jensen & Nickelsen, 2008). In fact, the National Reading Panel (2002) identifies this as one of seven scientifically based research strategies that improve reading comprehension. The act of creating questions about what is being read focuses the students' attention on the content as well as their metacognition about the content and their reading accuracy. The CCSS ask us to take students on a journey with complex text, and questioning strategies will be an imperative part of that.

Preparation and Materials

Create four Quad Cards for each student. We suggest giving students question stems from Zone 2 on page 90 so they can more easily grasp the idea of creating their own questions.

Ask students to cut the cards apart so they each have four to exchange with others in their small group. Prepare text, video, or a website that students will use to create their questions.

Instructions

Place students in groups of five. Give each student four Quad Cards. Use this strategy after you have read a book, listened to a minilesson, or watched a video. Students then create four higher-level questions based on the content. They should write each question in a different box.

Once the questions are written, the student writes his or her name within each box on the line marked "author 1" and gives the other four groupmates a question square. When all students in the group do this, each student will have four questions to answer. Next, each student answers all four questions and signs his or her name on the line marked "author 2" (see figure 7.3). The questions and their answers, along with feedback on the strength of the question, are returned to author 1, who reviews the accuracy of his or her groupmates' responses.

Author 1: Adrienne

Question: How can you explain the differences between fractions and decimals?

Answer: They are exactly the same actually, but the fraction has a numerator on top of the denominator. A fraction is easier for me to visualize since the whole is represented as the denominator and the part is the numerator. Decimals just explain what "part" of 100 the number is—that is hard for me to visualize.

Author 2: Raoul

Figure 7.3: Sample Quad Card exercise.

We encourage students to write questions that force the brain to infer from the text and show the evidence from the book when answering. Text-based questions and answers will be of utmost importance.

Assessment

There are several ways to assess this strategy.

- Have students evaluate one another's questions. You could create a rubric or a checklist of what type of questions you asked your students to write.

- Have students evaluate whether or not the questions were written at a particular level on Bloom's Taxonomy, if you make that one of the requirements.

- Have students evaluate the answer to see if it's correct. Give that student feedback on his or her answer. If incorrect, the student should correct it.

- Hold students accountable for working together, otherwise known as cooperative learning.

Younger students will most likely need question starters or stems for these activities. Group students so they are generating and answering questions in line with their background knowledge or readiness level based on preassessment results. It's great to have students with strong background knowledge together so their questions can challenge one another. Another differentiation technique is to have two squares with three students in a group rather than four squares and five students.

This cooperative learning activity is engaging, since students know they will get to evaluate each other's questions and answers. They love playing teacher. This is a great review activity after reading any type of text but especially after complex texts, since amazing conversations and clarifications might occur as well.

17. Reflective Conversations

The first Speaking and Listening anchor standard asks students to "prepare for and participate effectively in a range of conversations and collaborations with diverse partners, building on others' ideas and expressing their own clearly and persuasively" (CCRA.SL.1). Students will need to integrate and evaluate information that others present. The listening piece is the precursor to being able to speak appropriately. Reflective Conversations is designed to help students communicate their thoughts before the reading, during the reading, and after the reading, as well as to summarize, integrate, or evaluate their partners' responses.

Preparation and Materials

Give each student a Reflective Conversations With Nonfiction Checklist reproducible (page 118 or visit **go.solution-tree.com/commoncore** to download). Choose a nonfiction text, article, or essay to read. You'll need to create reflective questions for before, during, and after the reading. Or you can use our list of generic questions that we have provided (be aware, they might need to be adjusted slightly). The text can be any length, but you or your students will need to create stopping points for more lengthy text so that the students will know when to stop and ask the during-reading questions. To make sure all students have access to the questions, you can either write the questions on the SMART Board or print the generic list so they have a copy in front of them.

Instructions

Pair students up. There is no one way to group students for this activity; it will depend on their reading ability of text, ability to communicate and listen, social skills, level of support needed, and so on. Provide students with reflective questions for the various stages of reading, such as the following. (Visit **go.solution-tree.com /commoncore** to download these question lists.)

Before-reading questions:

- Look through the reading passage (pictures, graphs, bold headings, captions, and so on). What are some of the things that you already know about the passage? Have you experienced anything about this passage in your personal life? If so, please explain.

- What are some predictions about the main idea of the passage?

- What concepts are you trying to understand by reading this passage? (Look at any boldface type words within the passage and words within titles and headings.)

- What are your reading goals for this passage? (State your personal reading growth goal or purpose for reading this text.)

- What do you hope to learn by reading this passage?

- Name at least two strategies that you might use while reading this passage.

During-reading questions:

- Have your predictions about the main idea of this passage changed? Why, or why not?
- What reading strategies have been most helpful so far, and why?
- What are the important aspects of this passage so far? Please summarize.
- What questions do you have about the passage (interest based or for review)?
- What new vocabulary words came your way that you don't fully understand? (Take the time to find the meaning of these words.)

After-reading questions:

- How are you feeling about what you read? Any emotions about the passage?
- What was the main idea within the passage?
- What reading strategies did you find most helpful, and why?
- How do you see yourself using this information in future situations (school and family life)?
- What information really had an impact on you, and why?
- How can you summarize the reading passage in your own words?
- What new vocabulary words came your way that you don't fully understand? (Take the time to find the meaning of these words.)

Taking turns, one partner asks the other a before-reading question, a during-reading question, and an after-reading question at the appropriate times while reading a content area text. Students can also take turns reading the passages aloud so they can support each other. There might be a few students that you pull so they can read with you and receive your guidance and feedback. They should ask and respond to questions just like a conversation. To ensure accurate, active listening, have each student paraphrase how his or her partner answered the question. So Partner A asks a question, Partner B responds, and then Partner A rephrases the answer to make sure it is understood. Have students fill out the Reflective Conversations With Nonfiction Checklist reproducible as they assess whether the conversation is productive.

Assessment

There are many ways to assess this strategy.

- Choose a partnership to listen to and take observation notes.
- Have students write each other's responses on paper so they can evaluate the answer better (working memory tends to struggle with too much information).
- Have students write any disagreements they had on paper so everyone can discuss.
- Encourage students to use some of the unique vocabulary words that they come across in the reading while they are having the conversation. Students can note these neat opportunities at the bottom of their checklist.
- Have students document their reading goal and journal how they accomplished it.
- Review each student's Reflective Conversations With Nonfiction Checklist reproducible.

This strategy encourages good speaking, listening, and reading skills. We hope your students will enjoy it as much as ours have. The cognitive engagement levels during this activity are high, since students are reading complex texts; thinking about strategies before, during, and after; and assessing how the process is proceeding.

18. H Diagram

Comparing and contrasting terms, perspectives, characters, ideas, themes, and other concepts in all content areas is extremely powerful, because it forces the mind to interpret, evaluate, and conclude. According to Robert Marzano, Debra Pickering, and Jane Pollock (2001) in *Classroom Instruction That Works*, there is a 45 percentile point gain when students are asked to compare and contrast, sort, and classify. This strategy is short, powerful, and CCSS friendly. Reading anchor standards four and nine ask students to "interpret words and phrases as they are used in the text" (CCRA.R.4) and "analyze how two or more texts address similar themes or topics . . . or compare the approaches the authors take" (CCRA.R.9). Comparing and contrasting can help with this interpretation and analyzing.

If you choose to use words to compare and contrast (rather than books, authors, characters, and so on), remember to use Tier 2 words—general academic terms that can be used across the curricula—as much as possible.

Preparation and Materials

You'll need chart paper (for younger students) or construction paper. Also come up with two concepts, themes, author perspectives, vocabulary terms, or other categories for students to compare and contrast that go along with the curriculum. You have many choices with how you choose your terms:

- Give each partnership a different set of terms, concepts, or phrases to compare and contrast. You can cover more content this way.

- Give all partnerships the same set of words to compare and contrast. You can go into more depth with the content this way.

- Complete the process as a whole class with just two words, phrases, or concepts. Be sure to do this together the first time anyway to model how to use the H diagram.

Instructions

Have students create a gigantic, bubble-shaped *H* on chart paper, with chalk on the school playground, or with a large piece of construction paper.

Give them two concepts from your target to compare and contrast within this H diagram. The students label the top of each vertical line with a concept (see figure 7.4, page 108). The similarities go in the middle of the *H* (the crossbar connecting the two vertical lines), and the differences go under the concept they belong to within the two vertical lines. It's basically a Venn diagram with more space to write. Since the CCSS want evidence from text, remind students to record the page number next to their notes in the H diagram so they know where they found the information.

Always take time to have each small group share its H diagram via a quick presentation, a gallery walk where students walk around in small groups reading each H diagram and leaving a sticky note with comments or a question, or a whole-group discussion.

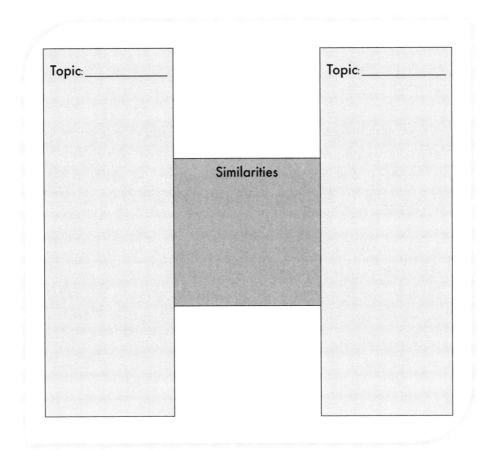

Figure 7.4: The H diagram.

Assessment

There are many ways to assess this strategy.

- Have students check whether the information within the diagram is correct. Were the pieces of information in the crossbar truly what the concepts had in common? Were the differences in the correct place? Did students prove their answers by placing page numbers from text that gave the information?

- Check how students went about finding the similarities and differences. Did they use viable resources, or did they guess?

- See whether students showed effort to understand the similarities and differences. For instance, can they verbally explain to others what they have written?

Because this activity is powerful and easy to use, students can engage in comparing and contrasting on a weekly basis.

19. Stump the Chump

This quick, easy-to-use questioning strategy is also a game (Jensen & Nickelsen, 2008). The point of the game is to promote the practice of answering questions from students' notes by having them show where they got their information. The CCSS are always emphasizing citing evidence, and Stump the Chump promotes this concept. Student teams ask questions of other teams in order to enhance their awareness of where the answer came from. The answers can come from a text, their notes (from videos, teacher, website, and so on), or handy electronics if available. This is a great way to review before a summative assessment.

Preparation and Materials

You'll need one index card per student and a text. Ask students to have their resources ready for use (notes from class, texts, technology, and so on). Students will need time to read and reread the assigned text and any notes from class.

Instructions

Divide students into groups of three or four. Groups should generate ten questions from the class discussion or from related texts. Questions should be of moderate difficulty, all short answer. For example, in a unit on drugs and their effects, good questions would be: What are three examples of a stimulant? How will a depressant affect your body? How do the narcotics morphine, heroin, and codeine affect your body? Encourage students to use the question stems from Zone 2 on page 90. Questions should be written in such a way that the person who answers (the chump) has to show where in the text or notes he or she learned that answer. Visit www.achievethecore.org to learn to write text-dependent questions.

Have students quiz each other within the groups to ensure everyone knows the questions and location of content prior to attempting to stump another group. Once everyone is ready, two groups come to the front of the class. Divide the rest of the class in half temporarily so that each group has its own cheering gallery. Each group then takes turns directing their ten questions to the leader (chump) of the other group, trying to stump him or her. The chump answers and shows where he or she studied that information from the text and notes. Chumps can get a lifeline from their teammates if they wish—group members can help with location of content and answers. The group leader gets gallery cheers when he or she answers correctly. When all ten questions are done from each group, two new groups of students come up front.

Ensure that every student has the opportunity to represent his or her group and each student has the opportunity to cheer a teammate on. Rotate leadership roles after a round of questions or when you do this activity in the future.

Assessment

Use this checklist to assess this strategy:

- Student questions vary from lower-level recall questions to higher-level thinking questions.
- The questions are focused on the topic and do not stray.
- The questions are text dependent.
- All students participate in the creation of the questions.
- The chump can show where the information is located in the text or notes.

This fun game is sure to engage brains at higher levels. Everyone likes to try to stump the chump.

Conclusion

This chapter has introduced both long-term research strategies and daily exploration strategies, all of which engage the brain at higher levels. They help students master the Common Core standards focused on researching, exploring, and deepening understanding of the content introduced in Zone 1.

Now on to the grand finale—Zone 3: Engage to Own. These next two chapters will prepare students to argue, debate, question other opinions, and formulate stronger self-efficacy.

ASQ Time

1. **Action step:** What is the single most valuable next step you will take after having read this chapter?

2. **Summary of learning:** Summarize in three to five sentences what you learned in this chapter.

3. **Question:** What discussion questions do you have for other readers, for the authors, or for self-reflection to explore more from this chapter?

Brainstorming Bonanza

Topic: _____

Step 1: List potential sources in the appropriate category.

Internet (websites, blogs, Twitter)	Print (books, journals, magazines)	People (experts, relatives, classmates)

Step 2: List subtopics around the topic like a web.

Topic: _____

Step 3: Circle the subtopics of interest.

Brainstorming Bonanza Checklist

☐ I have at least three different sources from each category that I can use for brainstorming subtopics.

☐ I did some preliminary research to determine my subtopics that are within the web.

☐ I believe my subtopics are appropriate and accurate for this larger topic.

☐ I narrowed down which subtopics I will include in my future research.

Credible and Accurate Resource Tracker

Name of researcher: _____

Research topic: _____ Date: _____

RESOURCE INFORMATION (MLA style)	CREDIBILITY RANKING AND EXPLANATION 1 = Not very credible 2 = Credible 3 = Very credible	INFORMATION USED FROM THIS RESOURCE (quotes and page numbers)	INTEGRATION OF INFORMATION (paraphrasing, direct quote, block quote)	NEW QUESTIONS

Different Perspectives

Name of researcher: _____

RESOURCE 1	RESOURCE 2	RESOURCE 3
Cite it:	Cite it:	Cite it:
Important ideas and perspectives on topic: • • •	Important ideas and perspectives on topic: • • •	Important ideas and perspectives on topic: • • •
My response to this perspective:	My response to this perspective:	My response to this perspective:

My conclusion on the credibility of the above resources is (write on the back of page, if necessary):

Presentation Rubric: Primary (Grades K–3)

Directions: Circle the level that best describes how you performed for each criterion. Feel free to explain your choice in the margin.

CRITERIA	LEVEL 1	LEVEL 2	LEVEL 3	LEVEL 4
I stayed on topic during my presentation.	Rarely	Sometimes	Often	Always
I explained my thoughts and ideas by myself.	I needed a lot of help from the teacher or my classmates.	I needed some help from the teacher or my classmates.	I needed a little help from the teacher or my classmates.	I did it by myself.
I changed my voice in different ways.	I didn't change my voice. I was monotone.	I changed my voice a little bit.	I often changed my voice.	I always changed my voice.
I used my body to make my message clear (used hands, stepped in different directions, nodded head, pointed fingers, and so on).	I didn't use my body to make my message clear.	I sometimes used my body to make my message clear.	I often used my body to make my message clear.	I always used my body to make my message clear.
I encouraged and responded to comments and questions.	Rarely	Sometimes	Often	Always

What did you do well in your presentation?

_____

_____

What can you do next time to improve your presentation?

_____

_____

Presentation Rubric: Intermediate (Grades 4–8)

Student presentation skill goal: _____

Evaluator: For each category, please circle the box that best explains the presenter's presentation skills. Add the number of points and record in the grade summary section at the bottom of the rubric. Feel free to write comments about the categories within the specific category box.

	NEEDS IMPROVEMENT *1 point*	GOOD *2 points*	EXCELLENT *3 points*
Organization	Grabber, conclusion, or sequence not strong or evident	Sequence is not logical, but grabber and conclusion present	Sequence is coherent and easy to follow; outstanding grabber and conclusion
Content	Important information not mentioned; no clear purpose; standards not evident; nonexistent or very weak arguments; main ideas unclear	Some important information emphasized; some content goes along with the standards; arguments a little weak; some main ideas clear	Most important information present; content goes along with the standards; strong arguments supported content; main ideas clear
Facial Expression	Little to no facial expressions	Some facial expressions kept audience engaged	Lots of facial expressions showed the emotion of the content; facial expressions helped communicate the content better
Gestures	Little to no gestures	Some gestures clearly planned to better emphasize the content	Arms, stance, hands, head, and body movement used throughout presentation to convey importance of content

page 1 of 2

	NEEDS IMPROVEMENT *1 point*	GOOD *2 points*	EXCELLENT *3 points*
Eye Contact	Little eye contact with participants; eyes mostly on notes or elsewhere	Some eye contact used in appropriate places within the presentation	Eye contact strong; student knew material well enough to look at audience the majority of the time
Vocal Expression	Very little vocal expression; monotonous voice	Some vocal expression	Variations in vocal tone, pitch, and speed; encouraged participant engagement

Grade summary: _____

Student's strengths:

Suggestions:

Feedback about goal:

Possible goals for next presentation:

Jensen, E., & Nickelsen, L. (2008). Deeper learning: 7 powerful strategies for in-depth and longer-lasting learning. *Thousand Oaks, CA: Corwin Press.*

Reflective Conversations With Nonfiction Checklist

Place a checkmark in Partner A's box and/or Partner B's box after he or she gives evidence of fulfilling the criteria described. Give proof in the comments box. Since there are several questions and opportunities to respond to the reading, there will be several checks in each box.

Partner A's Name: _____   Partner B's Name: _____

CRITERIA	PARTNER A	PARTNER B	COMMENTS
Student appropriately answered the questions and gave evidence from the text to support answer.			
Student communicated the answer effectively, clearly, and accurately.			
Student actively listened by summarizing what speaker said, challenging the speaker if he or she disagreed, asking clarifying questions if he or she did not understand the answer, or responding to what was said.			

CHAPTER 8

ZONE 3: ENGAGE TO OWN

When information has become part of you, you live it, breathe it, talk about it, think about it, and can argue about it. It is not only in your long-term memory, but it's also in your blood. This is a whole different level of understanding content. Students acquired simple information in Zone 1: Engage to Build Basics, had their curious phase in Zone 2: Engage to Explore, and now, in Zone 3, students will grapple with content in such a way that they will eventually *own* it.

Zone 3: Engage to Own is the love-of-learning zone, where students express what they learned in different, more in-depth ways. They talk about it with passion. They take action, using what they learned to make a difference in others' lives and their own.

Getting students to think at complex, yet doable, levels is the goal of this engagement zone. In *College and Career Ready*, David Conley (2010) states that there are five key cognitive skills that college-bound students should be proficient in when entering college. They are at the heart of how postsecondary educators think and teach. In other words, every entry-level college course across the disciplines is embedded with these key cognitive skills:

- *Problem formulation.* The student develops and applies multiple strategies to formulate routine and nonroutine problems and uses method-based approaches for complex problems. The student develops a repertoire of strategies . . .

- *Research.* The student identifies appropriate resources to help answer a question or solve a problem by identifying all possible sources . . .

- *Interpretation.* The student analyzes competing and conflicting descriptions of an event or issue to determine the strengths and flaws in each . . . ; synthesizes the results of an analysis . . . ; states the interpretation that is . . . most reasonable based on available evidence; and presents orally or in writing an extended description, summary, and evaluation . . .

- *Communication.* The student constructs well-reasoned arguments or proofs to explain phenomena or issues . . . , accepts critiques of or challenges to assertions, and addresses critiques and challenges by providing a logical explanation or refutation . . .

- *Precision and accuracy.* The student knows what type of precision is appropriate to the task and the subject area . . . [and] is able to increase precision and accuracy through successive approximations generated from a task or process that is repeated . . . The student applies understanding of content knowledge appropriately and accurately, achieves accurate results, and reaches appropriate conclusions. (Conley, 2010, p. 34)

One way to achieve this goal of complex thinking is through "close reading," which is the act of investigating a short piece of text with multiple readings over multiple instructional lessons while unraveling the rich meaning. Close reading demands that students interpret the text, communicate their opinions about the text, and apply their understanding of what was learned from the reading based on what was inferred or what the author said. These are just a few of the ways close reading of complex text prepares students for college texts and content.

Close Reading

The CCSS require close reading of complex texts to both determine what the text says explicitly and make logical inferences in narratives and nonfiction. Reading anchor standard one says that students will be able to "read closely to determine what the text says explicitly and to make logical inferences from it; cite specific textual evidence when writing or speaking to support conclusions drawn from the text" (CCRA.R.1). Reading anchor standard ten says that students will be able to "read and comprehend complex literary and informational texts independently and proficiently" (CCRA.R.10). Combine these two standards and you have a very intense, rigorous reading opportunity. Improving comprehension of complex texts will make the content more meaningful and, therefore, more memorable.

Douglas Fisher (2013) defines close reading as

an instructional approach that requires readers to re-read a text several times and really develop a deep understanding of the content contained in the text. The purpose is to build the habits of readers as they engage with the complex texts and to build their stamina and skills for being able to do so independently. However, close reading doesn't mean that you simply distribute a complex reading and then exhort them to read it again and again until they understand it. As part of a close reading, students "read with a pencil" and learn to annotate as they go. In addition, they are asked text-dependent questions that require that they produce evidence from the text as part of their responses.

As Fisher mentions, close reading entails using a pencil. Writing thoughts while reading is an extremely powerful strategy used during the reading process. In her book *So What Do They Really Know?*, Cris Tovani (2011) says that when students annotate challenging text, they are writing reactions, questions, and opinions; making connections; and predicting what might be coming up in the text. These thoughts make for rich discussions too. When students annotate, they are forced to pay close attention to details and begin thinking with the author about the evidence.

We can parse out several specific targets to help students achieve these standards, such as analyze vocabulary and how its meaning is shaped by context; analyze the form, tone, imagery, and figurative language; determine the significance of word choice and syntax; logically argue and critique the reasoning of authors; glean evidence from text; apply critical thinking skills; and discover the different levels of meaning as passages are read multiple times. When using the Zone 3 strategies in the next chapter to help students reach these targets, it is important for teachers to aim toward a gradual release of responsibility, so students eventually engage in close reading independently.

We do know that when students are reading complex texts and fulfilling Reading anchor standards one and ten, we should not build their background knowledge as much or use too many prereading strategies; rather, students will gain background knowledge from the first reading and comprehend the text more deeply after subsequent readings. The CCSS want all students to productively struggle with complex texts. This zone will provide you with several of the best strategies and tools to help students achieve deeper understandings of complex texts. They really own the text more when close reading occurs.

Here are some questions and question stems to help you create opportunities for student thinking during your lessons. Place your content strategically within these question stems to formulate a question that helps the students own the content or skill. At this level, questions should elicit emotional responses in many situations.

- Do you agree or disagree with _____, and why?

- How would you justify, rate, evaluate, and defend the importance of _____?

- Which is better, and which is worse?

- How would you prioritize or rank _____?

- Which solution is the best, and why?

- Does this compete with any values you hold? Which ones? How?

- How did you feel about learning this?

- What are the most important things that you have learned to date? Are there things you would now do differently if you could repeat the experience, and if so, why? How differently do you see your future role as a learner in light of what you've learned?

- Does this validate or repudiate anything you know?

- How will you take this and grow from it?

- In light of what you have learned so far, what are your learning priorities for the next few weeks? How can you build on what you have learned? What new knowledge and understanding do you hope to acquire? What new skills do you need to develop? What can you do to ensure that you don't lose sight of these targets?

- Why should you teach this information to someone else?

- What knowledge gaps are you aware of now that you've explored the content?

These questions are at the heart of learning. We hope students become passionate about the topics embedded into these question stems and want to own them!

When to Use Zone 3

After students have studied basic information and explored it at deeper levels, they are ready to engage to own. Close reading provides students with multiple opportunities to understand a text at deeper levels since rereading will occur. Each reading builds more background knowledge for the reader.

Zone 3 is perfect for when standards require students to do the following things:

- Solve real problems within the world, community, school, classroom, or home
- Predict how the world might respond to certain actions
- Demonstrate a skill or process
- Invent something for the benefit of specific locations or a group of people or even just one person
- Apply what they know to a new situation
- Transfer knowledge into a new context
- Create and apply new ideas
- Debate or passionately state an opinion with supporting details

How to Build a Zone 3 Target

As stated in previous chapters, powerful targets have three pieces: Do, Know, and Show. The Do is the verb for student thinking, the Know is the specific content or skill students need to master, and the Show is how they prove they completed the target. Here is a list of Zone 3 verbs and verb phrases that you could use in your target to engage students to own the content:

- Apply the skills learned to the classroom assignment and in different contexts
- Use the content so that a solution can be created
- Get others involved in order to implement a plan of action
- Apply information at the personal, local, national, or international level
- Decide how this information can benefit others
- Change the content into a different form (from picture or graphic to writing, from writing to speaking, from direct quote to paraphrased text)
- Create a theory and be able to support it
- Debate or share opinions with support on a topic
- Explain, summarize, or paraphrase using additional ideas from your own experience or other sources
- Use higher-level vocabulary words correctly to express the learning
- Set goals for future learning
- Empathize with situations and others' perspectives
- Listen with understanding and empathy and then summarize what was said
- Think about your own thinking; be able to explain your thinking processes
- Read closely
- Examine phrases and words
- Ask the author questions

Your Do will be a Zone 3 verb or verb phrase from this list. Your Know will be more complex content gleaned from closely reading complex text or reflecting on what was learned based on your chosen standard.

Finally, it's time to decide on your Show, which is the product your students will create to prove they can think about the content at the required level, all while using the criteria for success.

Conclusion

Now that you have a strong understanding of close reading to help your students be successful at comprehending complex texts, let's explore Zone 3 close reading strategies as well as daily, quick strategies that keep students highly engaged throughout the whole lesson.

ASQ Time

1. **Action step:** What is the single most valuable next step you will take after having read this chapter?

2. **Summary of learning:** Summarize in three to five sentences what you learned in this chapter.

3. **Question:** What discussion questions do you have for other readers, for the authors, or for self-reflection to explore more from this chapter?

CHAPTER 9

STRATEGIES FOR ZONE 3

Complex texts are extremely rich in content, and students will need a couple of readings, deep discussions, and powerful, high-cognitive engagement in order to comprehend them. Thus, this chapter focuses on eleven Zone 3: Engage to Own strategies—seven for longer-term close reading targets and four that can be implemented in daily lessons. The strategies explored here are among the best. They take the brain to levels of thinking that the other zones do not. While you read through them, we hope you see the level of ownership one takes on while participating in these activities.

Close Reading Strategies

Following are seven strategies for implementing close reading so all students will be successful with complex texts in all content areas: Close Reading Steps, Close Reading Marks, Three Short Summaries for Nonfiction, Fix-It Activities, Reciprocal Teaching With Nonfiction, Mindmapping for Solutions, and Stop-n-Think.

20. Close Reading Steps

The CCSS ask students to perform close reading of complex texts more often in order to achieve the levels of mastery the standards require. Close Reading Steps makes the process easier.

Preparation and Materials

The timeline for preparation is days or even weeks before a close read. Become familiar with the steps of close reading so you can model the process smoothly. Choose between one and three reading strategies (such as predicting, summarizing, or questioning) that you will model and want your students to use during reading (don't assume they know the strategy or skill). Be sure to review the Reading anchor standards and include your grade-level specific standards. Teach the strategies, model the strategies (think aloud), and gradually release the responsibility with these strategies using texts other than the one you are using for your complex text lesson.

Reading strategies that you can teach and model include:

- Clarifying
- Comparing and contrasting

- Connecting to prior knowledge

- Inferring (generalizing and drawing conclusions)

- Predicting

- Questioning the text

- Recognizing the author's purpose

- Seeing causal relationships

- Summarizing

- Visualizing

Choose a one-page text that supports your outcome and meets the criteria for *complex*. Copy this short text or section for all students since they will be writing on it (to save paper, you can place the text in slip covers and give students dry-erase markers to mark the text).

Guide each reading by setting its purpose for each reading ahead of time. To set the purpose, use Reading anchor standards two through nine. For example, the first read should be about the first domain, Key Ideas and Details, which covers anchor standards two and three. The second read can focus on the craft and structure of the text using anchor standards four through six. The third read can focus on the integration of knowledge and ideas by using anchor standards seven through nine. You certainly don't need to cover all the anchor standards with one close read; you will have many opportunities to use these standards during close reading throughout the year.

When creating text-dependent questions, make sure you promote gradual but deep analysis of the text. The set of questions after each read should be geared toward the purposes you chose and should ease students into higher-level thinking and a deeper understanding of the text. Basic questions at the beginning are totally appropriate. Ensure that students are backing their answers with evidence.

Instructions

Tell the students what close reading is and why it's important for lifelong reading success. Remind them that complex texts require close reading in order to analyze and comprehend them deeply. They can't just read these texts like they would a book on their reading level that they are highly interested in. The students need to understand why reading complex texts is important and how it helps them become better prepared for college texts, readies them for thinking processes in real life, and helps them think at high levels that improve overall processing skills.

There are so many ways to closely read a text. It will depend on your text, your students' reading levels, their background knowledge, how much time you have, and your purposes for the close read. This is an approach with many choices.

First Read

Share the targets with your students for this lesson. Make sure the purposes for this first reading are very clear.

Students then preview the text on their own, looking at title, author, captions, pictures, chapter titles, subheadings, and so on. Remind them to use good prereading strategies, but don't do it for them.

Next, students read the text through for the first time. If students really struggle, partner them up or pull a small group together and read together. Have students mark confusing words, phrases, or sections in pencil during this time too. Use your text-dependent questions to help them focus on the purposes for reading the text, and make sure they know where in text their answer originates. After this first read, determine the main idea or the gist of the passage. (If they cannot, start the second read. While annotating, they might figure it out.)

Students could then discuss with a partner interesting facts, main ideas, or difficult sections. There should always be some kind of turn-and-talk discussion after each read to help clarify sections of texts.

Second Read

Center this second reading on how the author says what he or she is writing about. It's time to go deeper. Students should focus on how the words, sentences, and paragraphs shape the meaning or tone of text. The second read can be a total reread of the whole text or just a partial read of targeted sections.

Before this step, it's important to discuss annotations in small groups. Teacher-created questions that require text-based answers will be important during the discussion. Finally, asking students to create their own summary will be of utmost importance.

At this point, students start to annotate the text with pencil. Give students ideas of what to annotate based on what you know about the text, the target, and what strategies you have modeled. There are three types of annotations:

1. **Open annotation**—Allow students to annotate any thoughts that come to their mind while reading. These students have shown you they are strategic readers and know when and how to choose reading strategies.

2. **Guided annotation**—Invite students to use two to three specific annotation marks that you know they need to grow in, but also allow them to choose other annotation marks that they feel comfortable with. These students have shown you that they are strategic readers with certain skills but have some growth opportunities as well. Be close by so you can guide them if they get stuck.

3. **Closed annotation**—Give students about two to four ways to annotate while reading. Be specific with instructions, such as: circle unknown words, underline confusing sections and place a question mark next to this section of text, and guess the meanings of words next to the circled words. These students struggle with reading strategies and need explicit guidance and instruction during the annotation process. You might want to sit next to this group of students, since they will need more guidance than other groups.

Following are some potential annotations to choose from when responding in writing:

- Highlight repeated words in order to predict the main idea better.
- Write a summary after each paragraph or subheading within the margin of paper near the section (if needed).
- Generate questions while reading, and then write them near the section.
- Draw a picture or symbol of a word that you need to understand better.
- Write the definition of an unknown word based on context clues or a dictionary definition.
- Asterisk the most important facts.
- Include numbers to sequence events.
- Circle new words or unique words.

- Mark slang words, innuendoes, puns, figurative language, and irony that create the tone or mood of the text.

- Determine how the passage is organized.

- Note special meter, rhythm, rhymes, onomatopoeias, and so on.

- Agree or disagree with the author—what is his or her attitude toward the subject and readers? What does this passage tell us about the author?

- Create an analogy or connection to a particular section.

- Document new information to you and record aha! moments.

- Explain why you might have laughed.

- Mark contradictions within the text.

- Mark sections that you reread.

- Write down themes that the details are pointing toward.

- Mark patterns from passage to passage. Did you notice any repetitions and similarities from one section of the text to another one?

After the second read, students can collaborate with one another to share their annotations and their answers to the text-dependent questions. Ask students text-dependent questions that help them reread to find the answer, be able to give the page number or section number, and give the evidence for the answer.

Third Read

The purpose of the third read is to go deeper. Students should be evaluating the quality and value of the text and comparing it to other texts.

Determine if a third read is needed. Are there more in-depth meanings of the text that need to be discussed and explored? Are there still clarifying questions being asked? Is there another layer of the onion that needs to be peeled back? Is fluency with the text improving among students? Did you observe deeper comprehension during the second read?

Assessment

This close reading process should show that students reached the targets of the lesson, gained deep insights and understanding from the text, and accomplished the purposes of the readings.

There are several ways to assess this strategy.

- Have students evaluate one another and create a checklist of purposes for the reading. After the purposes have been discussed and implemented, students can check the box and explain how they accomplished the goal for each read.

- Challenge students to know their Lexile level of reading, and set goals to improve it each month. All students should be growing as readers, and a documented Lexile score is strong evidence. (See www.lexile.com for more information.)

- Use Reading anchor standards two through eight to achieve the close reading with complex texts. They all help the student closely examine text in different ways.

- Center your evidence-based questions carefully on your targets for that reading when assessing the comprehension of complex texts.

- Use your Cruisin' Clipboard to determine who is comprehending the texts at the deep level.

- Examine the students' annotations to determine their thought processes during the close read.

There are also several ways to differentiate this strategy. Complex texts will most likely be above students' independent reading level. When you are planning a close read with complex text, you will probably want all students to have the same text, although you don't need to all the time. Reading the same book builds community and deep discussion with all students. There will be some students who will struggle through the first read and get the gist of it, but many won't be able to understand the majority of the words. Kylene Beers and Robert Probst (2013), in their book *Notice and Note*, explain the type of support we might need to give: "Whichever book you ultimately choose to share with a group, be prepared to help students through it in multiple ways. . . . You'll read aloud some of it to them; they might listen to some of it on tape; they might buddy read" (pp. 49–50). The bottom line is this: give students the support they need to understand what the text is saying or they will abandon it, tune you out, or worse yet, start to hate reading. Help them be successful in *any* way possible.

One technique to help students is to do a mini-think-aloud for a section of confusing text so they can share strategies, thoughts, and questions that arise while reading.

Students could also construct a thesis based on all the detailed information they found and their annotations. This thesis could be used to prove to students that they could actually write argumentative papers.

Invite students to generate their own questions during the readings. When students generate questions while reading, it improves comprehension. This can be done by marking confusing sections of the text, rereading that section, and then creating questions about it. You can collect and list these questions, ask students to try to answer them in small groups, and then discuss them as a whole group (Beers & Probst, 2013).

Although close reading is a rather new strategy for many educators (despite being around since 1929), it can be taught and loved. Students will become more confident readers as they use this powerful strategy to tackle complex texts.

21. Close Reading Marks

In this strategy, students will use CCSS-friendly symbols to document their metacognition with the text they are reading (fiction or nonfiction). They can flag a book, article, or photocopied pages with symbols of thinking written directly on copied text or on sticky notes and placed on the page where the thought occurred. Later, these notes will be used for writing and discussions. Close Reading Marks is a stepping stone for annotating.

Preparation and Materials

Copy the Close Reading Marks reproducible (page 153 or visit **go.solution-tree.com/commoncore** to download) for each student. Then choose a complex text that fits your grade level and your standards. For text exemplars for each grade level and genre, see the CCSS appendix B (NGA & CCSSO, n.d.a).

Instructions

Using your chosen complex text, determine which specific targets you want your students to focus on during the close reading. After previewing the text, you should be able to determine which symbols your students can use while reading. We suggest two symbols for younger students and three to five symbols for older students.

Decide whether you will photocopy the text so that students can write these symbols and their thoughts directly next to the words or if they will use sticky notes to document their symbols and thoughts in a book. Then follow the close reading steps from the previous strategy in conjunction with the symbols.

For the first read, students should read the text individually unless they need to engage with a partner. You could even help students engage with this text by reading it aloud to a small group.

For the second read, model use of the marks by sharing your thoughts about the text while reading and focusing on the specific targets you have chosen. Show and explain to students how you mark the text with your symbols while writing notes that explain both your thoughts and why you chose those symbols; you can use a document camera for this task.

Periodically stop to ask text-based questions (see page 20 to learn how to create these questions) so students prove their answers with evidence from text. Encourage discussion in small groups, partners, and the whole class.

Students should eventually read independently. Once you have gradually released the responsibility to the students and they have shown understanding of this strategy, they can practice using Close Reading Marks on their own. Remember to partner students with one another in order to share their thoughts and tags—one student reads his or her sticky notes to the other reading partner, and vice versa. When the sharing is over, ask students to take the sticky notes off the book pages and staple them together or place them on lined paper so you can read them and assess the metacognition.

Assessment

Create a checklist with questions similar to the following for you to use or for students to self-evaluate or evaluate a partner:

- Do the symbols match the comment or thought on the note?
- Did the student comprehend the text correctly? Can the student summarize the text in his or her own words?
- Did the student use the tags to contribute ideas and thoughts during the discussion?
- Did the student focus on the targets during the reading?
- Did the student go beyond those targets and find other thoughts and ideas to share?

To differentiate and extend this strategy, ask students to take two discussion pieces and elaborate with writing. Be sure you have criteria for success (what is expected as evidence of learning) ready—for instance, a rubric would work for a writing piece.

22. Three Short Summaries for Nonfiction

The Common Core Reading anchor standard two asks students to "summarize the key supporting details and ideas" from a text (CCRA.R.2). During close reading, students will be stopping in particular places to summarize what they think the author meant, what just happened, how the details support the main idea, what was added to their existing comprehension, and so on. Summarizing is a key skill for the CCSS.

We have learned that students struggle with summarizing information, so here we provide you with three different ways they can summarize quickly: (1) author's main idea, (2) main idea table, and (3) paragraph equation. In general, many educators believe it is easier to summarize narratives or fictional stories, while the nonfiction texts are more challenging to summarize. Since students process information differently, why not give them a choice in how they summarize?

Preparation and Materials
Prepare a nonfiction text for students to read and to try a summarization activity with.

Instructions
After students have acquired information through reading the chosen text, ask students to choose one method to help them create a short summary of what was read. Make sure to model how to use each method before giving them the choice. You might even use a different one each day. Once again, gradually release responsibility before giving them this assignment independently.

Author's Main Idea
Students should take the information garnered from each of the following four steps and create a paragraph summarizing the most important information and giving the details that led them to this conclusion.

1. What do you think the author thought was the most important statement, idea, or main idea from this text? What did the author emphasize several times? How did the text begin, end, and extend in the middle?

2. What proof did the author leave to make this inference? What is the evidence in the text (list page numbers and explain)?

3. What are facts from the reading that support this main idea (list page numbers)?

4. How might this information impact you, your friends or family, townspeople, your country, or the world (*impact* can be a solution to a problem, ideas to improve communities, negative or positive reactions, and so on)? Be sure to end this summary with the impact this information has on others.

The criteria of success for this activity could be a topic sentence, two to four detail sentences supporting the main idea, and a closing sentence, all in a student's own words.

Main Idea Table
Some students prefer a visual to help them understand what a paragraph is about. In that vein, the main idea table (see figure 9.1, page 132) helps many students understand that the main idea or topic sentence of a paragraph will fall down if it doesn't have strong legs for support (Nickelsen, 2004). In other words, details in a paragraph support the main idea.

Show students several examples and then create some together by reading a nonfiction paragraph to see if the author followed the rule for a good paragraph (be aware, not all authors do this well). We encourage at least four legs or details to make the table sturdy.

Eventually, students will be ready to create a summary by reading the sections of a nonfiction article, determining the main idea, and filling in the graphic organizer accordingly.

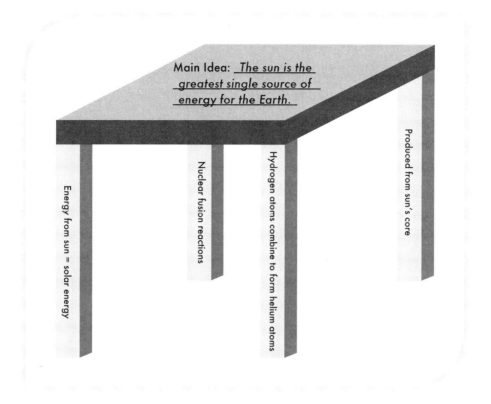

Figure 9.1: Main idea table example.

Paragraph Equation

For students who have a hard time determining the main idea of a longer passage, this summarization activity works well (Nickelsen, 2004). Students take a nonfiction article and number the paragraphs. They do a first read all the way through and infer what the author's main idea might be. Then, they use the paragraph equation to write down the topic sentence of each paragraph in the appropriate spot. After all the topic sentences are written down, the students read them aloud and determine what they all have in common. They then list the main idea of the passage at the bottom of the reproducible page. Have students double-check the main idea by rereading the title and the first and last paragraphs.

This is the beginning of a good summary. You could encourage the students to use some of the topic sentences they wrote down as details for this main idea.

Assessment

There are several ways to assess these summarization activities.

- Check whether the student used the steps correctly in the summary of his or her choice.

- Confirm that the students captured the gist of the text through this summary.

- Check whether the details for the summary were accurate. Did they really support the topic sentence of the summary?

- Confirm that the student used a concluding sentence to bring the pieces together.

By providing three summaries to choose from, you give students a higher probability for success and engagement with writing summaries for nonfiction text. Providing choices is a great example of differentiation: students get to the target in different ways and sometimes on different days.

For more ideas for main idea and summarization, see *Comprehension Mini-Lessons: Main Idea & Summarizing* (Nickelsen, 2004).

23. Fix-It Activities

Since students will be reading more complex texts, they will need to grapple with the text. They will probably need to "fix" their reading somehow. This quick list will be a great resource to use when it comes time for needing a reading strategy. The following quick reading remedies will help students while reading independently.

Preparation and Materials

Determine which Fix-It Activities are appropriate for your students. Also determine when to explain and model the activities. Eventually, place these activities on a poster so all students can see them while reading.

Instructions

Explaining and modeling the Fix-It Activities listed here is very important while students read from content area texts and even narratives. Create a shorter list from this inclusive list so students don't feel overwhelmed with choices.

- Reread tricky parts.
- Look for clues in the paragraph to help you figure out a tough word.
- Reread and try to visualize parts.
- Try rereading one or two sentences at a time, then retell these.
- Learn more about the content before reading further (build up background knowledge on the topic within the text).
- Self-monitor your reading by placing sticky notes in confusing text sections.
- Create questions for clarification.
- Make a connection between the text and your life, another text, or what you know about the world.
- Make a prediction.
- Stop and think about what you just read.
- Reflect in writing what you have read.
- Determine the patterns in the text structure.
- Adjust your reading rate: slow down or speed up.
- Read the section aloud.
- If none of the activities work, ask for help.

Assessment

Have students complete a comprehension self-assessment that might look like this:

- I am confused by _____ on page _____.

- I am confused because _____.

- I will try the following Fix-It Activity: _____.

- I now understand _____.

- I now have questions about _____.

Reading complex texts will definitely require a toolkit of powerful reading strategies to pull from when a reading struggle occurs. Many students know and use these skills automatically, but many still do not. This list will be a tool for them every time they read, and they will become better self-regulators in the reading process.

24. Reciprocal Teaching With Nonfiction

The CCSS ask students to work in small groups together so more speaking and listening skills are enhanced. They also ask students to summarize and question smaller sections of the text in more depth. Reciprocal Teaching With Nonfiction is an instructional procedure for teaching students to use multiple comprehension strategies flexibly and interactively in order to improve the learning of the content during content area reading. The process is simple: students take turns being the teacher, leading a dialogue about the text content with other students. The sheer challenge and complexity of this process almost force a deeper understanding.

Reciprocal teaching receives a staggering 0.74 effect size, suggesting it's a very smart strategy (Hattie, 2009). According to Hattie, the effect sizes tend to be higher when there is explicit teaching and practice of the cognitive strategies before beginning Reciprocal Teaching With Nonfiction dialogue (a gradual release of responsibility).

Preparation and Materials

First, choose a text for your students to discuss. You'll also need either the Reciprocal Teaching Cards: Primary (Grades K–3) reproducible (page 154) or the Reciprocal Teaching Cards: Intermediate (Grades 4–8) reproducible (page 156) for each group, depending on your students' grade level, and the Student Steps for Reciprocal Teaching reproducible (page 162) for each student. If you want students to document their conversations, provide them with the Reciprocal Teaching Conversation Notes reproducible (page 163). (Visit **go.solution-tree.com/commoncore** to download all reproducibles.)

Instructions

Explain Reciprocal Teaching With Nonfiction to the students by summarizing the four major roles in your own words.

1. **Predictor:** This role sets the purpose for reading.

2. **Clarifier:** This role helps students monitor their comprehension.

3. **Questioner:** This role increases students' awareness of the text's important ideas.

4. **Summarizer:** This role requires students to recall and arrange only the important ideas in a text.

We highly recommend that you take time to teach and model each of the four major roles (one role per week in primary grades, one per day in grades 4–8, two per day in high school). The predictor is the leader or teacher of the group, so make sure to meet with these leaders to ensure they understand the role.

You can also show YouTube videos of students at a similar grade level experiencing it. For instance, search "Reciprocal Teaching" on YouTube for primary classroom examples, and visit www.readingrockets.org /article/40008 for more ideas on how to introduce this very powerful reading strategy to primary students. (Visit **go.solution-tree.com/commoncore** for live links found in this text.)

The Student Steps for Reciprocal Teaching reproducible (page 162) is a great handout to give the students. We recommend using this handout only if you have modeled the process with them several times so they know what it looks and sounds like.

Assessment

There are several ways to assess Reciprocal Teaching With Nonfiction.

- Walk around while students are reading and discussing, and document comments that you hear to use for whole-group discussion.

- Have students complete a Reciprocal Teaching Self-Assessment Form reproducible (page 164 or visit **go.solution-tree.com/commoncore** to download).

- Encourage and give positive feedback to students as you see or hear them diving deeply into the text with powerful dialogue.

To differentiate and enrich this strategy, branch out to other roles such as the Connector, the Illustrator, the Wonderer, and the Noticer, all of which are featured on page 159.

Reciprocal Teaching With Nonfiction may well be one of the most powerful, engaging strategies that help students achieve many of the state standards in Reading, Writing, and Speaking and Listening. It takes time to develop these skills, especially to the point where students can perform independently. Don't give up— every minute of repeatedly modeling this strategy is worth it.

25. Mindmapping for Solutions

Twenty-first century skills are a big part of the CCSS. One aspect of 21st century thinking is giving students opportunities to be creative with the content they are learning. We have used mindmapping in our classrooms and workshops for years and continue to get great results and feedback from our learners. Students say that they enjoyed this learning process and didn't want to stop. Mindmapping for Solutions is a strategy that helps students take chaotic information from all kinds of sources and make meaningful chunks of information they can remember, speak about, and therefore, own.

Mindmapping is one of those all-encompassing strategies for the CCSS, since you can take this strategy to all areas of listening, speaking, writing, and reading. For example, our students eventually use their mindmaps to guide them during a speech they deliver. We have also used mindmaps as a way to brainstorm before writing, which goes along with Writing anchor standard two: "Write informative/explanatory texts to examine and convey complex ideas and information clearly and accurately through the effective selection, organization, and analysis of content" (CCRA.W.2). Similarly, Reading anchor standards two and five ask students to "determine central ideas of themes of a text and analyze their development" (CCRA.R.2) and "analyze the structure of texts, including how specific sentences, paragraphs, and larger portions of the text relate to each other and the whole" (CCRA.R.5). Mindmapping is a way to achieve these standards.

Preparation and Materials

Make sure to have colored pencils to add color to the mindmap and large white paper or chart paper.

Instructions

Mindmapping is just like webbing with a few extras—like color, images, and text—emphasized. While students are reading, learning, or reviewing content, they place the information in similar groupings or chunks. These chunks are like subheadings of smaller topics that stem from the main idea (see figure 9.2).

Figure 9.2: Mindmapping example of Italy.

Source: Keaton Nickelsen. Used with permission.

Students should first write their main topic in the center of the paper. Then direct students to use the following mindmap characteristics:

- Cluster or group similar facts related to the main topic.

- Use arrows or underlining to highlight the important ideas.

- Represent related topics in spokes around the main topic.

- Draw pictures or symbols to represent what you're learning (or include images from the Internet).

- Add plenty of color using colored pencils or skinny markers, because it enhances memory.

- Write short phrases and major concepts rather than sentences.

When students get good at this process, they can create mindmaps using software by Inspiration. (Visit www .inspiration.com for more information.)

There are so many ideas on how to organize content, but we wanted to focus on problem and solution since this is a powerful Zone 3 thinking process (see figure 9.3).

Students then research several of their subtopics. Students can share their maps with minipresentations, writing pieces, or even some type of drama. We need to involve students in many more real-world problems and solutions.

Assessment

There are several ways you can assess mindmap creation.

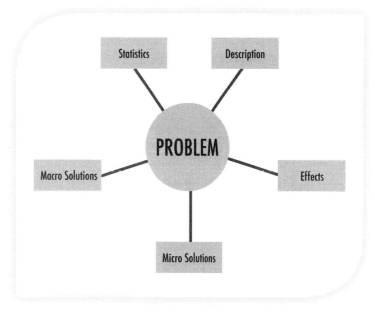

Figure 9.3: Sample problem and solution mindmap.

- Create a list of criteria for success characteristics for the mindmap, and have students self-assess at both the middle of the mindmapping project and at the end. We encourage you to check in the middle of the process and give students rich feedback. You can use the characteristics listed previously to help you create this list.

- Decide how the students will share these masterpieces: hang them in the hallway, present them in front of the classroom, write an argument, create an essay about the topic that was mindmapped, or design a product around the information researched. Make sure the requirements have been clearly identified and shared with the students.

Be aware that this is a highly engaging activity that students will thoroughly enjoy but also be challenged with—they may not want to stop. Use it monthly in different ways to keep deeper learning alive in your classroom.

26. Stop-n-Think

This powerful thinking process is easy to manage and informs instruction by student self-assessment, peer assessment, and teacher checks (Jensen & Nickelsen, 2008). Students will process chunks of information while acquiring information through reading texts or articles so there is greater understanding of the concept. This activity supports Writing anchor standard ten—"Write routinely over extended time frames (time for research, reflection, and revision) and shorter time frames (a single sitting or a day or two) for a range of tasks, purposes, and audiences" (CCRA.W.10)—since there will be shorter writing opportunities for a variety of purposes and tasks, as well as all ten of the Reading anchor standards depending on the route you take. Amazing, eh?

Preparation and Materials

Copy the Stop-n-Think With Checkpoints reproducible (page 167). This template is more for grades 3–8. It is used for learning chunks while the teacher is teaching minilessons, while reading smaller sections of text, or while viewing a video in short sections.

If you have younger students, copy one Stop-n-Think for Primary Students reproducible (page 168) per student. This template helps the primary students chunk and summarize a story in its three sections: beginning, middle, and end.

For each of the four boxes in the reproducible graphic organizer, create questions focused on a particular section of the text, depending on what you are teaching. We suggest downloading the template at **go.solution -tree.com/commoncore** and customizing it with your own questions. The sky is the limit with this activity.

Instructions

Teach students how to use the Stop-n-Think reproducible by having them process the text with the reproducible in front of them.

In box 1, teach the students the purpose of Stop-n-Think. One way to introduce the strategy is to present it in this way (Jensen & Nickelsen, 2008, p. 191):

- The brain can only pay attention for so long before it needs to stop and think about what was just said, heard, or seen. When the teacher is finished teaching why Stop-n-Think is so important, then students get to respond to this section or chunk of learning in a particular way . . . in box 1.
- Learning doesn't come in the lecture or video of the content. Learning comes in the processing of the content, in the thinking of what was just learned. Thinking can be in the form of personal reflection through writing, drawing, webbing, or discussing what was learned. After each chunk of content, students have the opportunity to write, draw, or web what they just learned in a particular box.
- When the lesson has been completed, students have the opportunity to process all of the pieces from the lesson by examining each chunk and tying them all together. The last box in the Stop-n-Think will be the summary box of what students learned.

When all students have written their responses, have them share what they wrote with a partner. If they like what their partner wrote, they can add that comment to their own box in another color of ink or pencil.

For box 2 of this strategy, we suggest you find video clips and create purpose questions to match your content. Be sure to view the video in advance so that you know where to pause or stop so that students can respond to the purpose question about the chunk they just saw. Make sure to share the purpose questions before showing the video; there should always be a purpose question before reading or viewing a video, otherwise, the brain might be more challenged to decipher what the most important information is. For example, if you're going to teach a lesson about biomes, give students your video-related purpose questions and play your selected video for about six to ten minutes. Then turn it off and ask students to answer the purpose questions ("What four biomes will we be studying in this unit? Give a characteristic of each.") in box 2.

Now invite students to read a specific passage in their texts. When they finish reading the chosen passage, they answer your reading-related questions in box 3. One differentiation technique is to list the questions on the dry-erase board and encourage students to choose one question to answer.

Invite students to write a summary of how Stop-n-Think boxes can benefit the learner in box 4.

In some lessons, you will only use two while in others you might create more boxes on the back of the reproducible. The idea is to let students experience learning in chunks and then process it in chunks before learning more. This way, the brain has the opportunity to remember information better than when each chunk is processed and partially consolidated. This process also allows us to check for understanding after each small chunk versus waiting until the end of the class and trying to figure out which step was not mastered.

Following are examples of Stop-n-Think for primary students (figure 9.4) and for upper-grade students (figure 9.5, page 140).

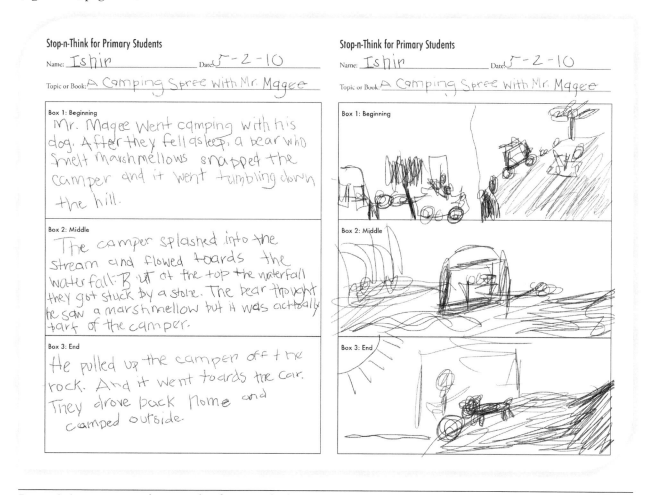

Figure 9.4: Primary-grade example of Stop-n-Think.

Following are some generic prompts for processing opportunities in Stop-n-Think:

- I have learned these new words: _____.

- I have learned these new facts: _____.

- I still have these questions: _____.

- The most valuable piece of information is _____.

- To summarize, I learned _____.

- The most important things to understand about _____ are _____.

- This concept is related to these other concepts: _____.

- When solving this math problem, remember to _____.

- The main idea of _____ is _____.

- The word _____ means _____.

- One event (use the exact words from text) to elaborate on is _____.

- An illustration of what I learned or visualized while reading is _____.

Name: Scott   Date: 2/18

Book: *Water—Shaping the Earth's Surface* (nonfiction)

Box 1: pp. 1–2 Define the difference between weathering and erosion in your own words.

Weathering happens when rock slowly wears away. Water is one cause of weathering. Chemicals in rain, ocean waves, and fast-flowing rivers slowly wear rock away. Erosion occurs after weathering. It occurs when water picks up worn-down rock particles and deposits them in other places.

Box 2: pp. 3–4 How does water specifically cause erosion?

Water can change earth by carving out canyons, valleys, and holes. Ocean waves and powerful rivers strike against rocks and soil, changing their space (weathering). Erosion occurs when water picks up the loose rocks.

Box 3: pp. 5–6 Compare and contrast a levee with a dam.

A levee is like a dam but is made of earth, rocks, stones, or sand. They both stop water flow after heavy rainfalls.

Box 4: pp. 7–8 What are some solutions to the massive amounts of flooding that occurs on Earth?

Building dams and flood control channels are two ways of decreasing the chances of flooding.

Synthesis of the boxes:

Weathering and erosion will continually occur on this Earth, but there are some solutions so that the damage is not so devastating to humans.

Figure 9.5: Upper-grade example of Stop-n-Think.

- I can solve this problem by _____.
- One example of how one event from the reading supports our theme of _____ is _____.
- Now that I have learned _____, I'm beginning to wonder _____.
- Some examples of _____ are _____.
- In my opinion, _____.
- I believe _____ is beneficial/harmful/dangerous because _____.
- I think _____ is necessary/unimportant because _____.
- I feel _____ is important because _____.
- I used to feel/believe _____, but now I feel/believe _____ because _____.
- Here is a possible way to solve the following problem: _____.

- Some details that I learned today are _____.
- I have the following questions that should help me understand _____ better.
- I made a personal connection with _____ because _____.

Assessment

There are a couple ways to assess a Stop-n-Think strategy.

- After students complete the warm-up in box 1, discuss their answers and ask students to self-assess by checking their level of mastery. This continues after each chunk of reading or learning content. Each stop helps students get closer to the challenging target. During your walkthrough, look for students who have checked Not Yet to show they don't understand the thinking opportunity. Help the student change this response to Need More Practice after reteaching or supplying a new strategy. Box 5 is reserved for the closure, summary of the big picture of the activity, or final demonstration of the target for that lesson. Every now and then, you should say: "I will check box numbers 3 and 5" to give the students a heads-up. In general, there should be a variety of checking on the part of the student, peer, and teacher.
- Create criteria for certain boxes that have more lengthy answers. Show the criteria to the students ahead of time and have them check to ensure they have those pieces before moving on to the next box.

To differentiate this strategy, encourage a variety of responses, such as complete sentences, webbing, drawing pictures, brainstorming words and their concepts, exact words from texts, and so on. You can also give students choices. After all, don't you appreciate choices in how you reflect on your learning? For instance, give students choices in how they summarize at the end: who, what, where, when, why, and how; the gist (a two-sentence summary); the main idea only; a sentence stem such as "_____ wanted to _____ but _____ so _____"; and so on. Other differentiation techniques include the following:

- Try giving some students more complex ways to process the content (higher-level questions, pros and cons, compare and contrast, arguments for and against, and so on).
- Provide smaller chunks of information to students who need it.
- Allow students to collaborate on the formation of their answers.
- If writing is challenging for the students, invite them to web or draw their learning.
- If students and teachers need more structure during the classroom time, use a Stop-n-Think that incorporates a warm-up and closure. A door pass is integrated into the template for this purpose.

This is an all-encompassing strategy that engages students at all levels of thinking; it just depends on how your target is written and how you form the Stop-n-Think. This strategy could cover almost all Reading and Writing anchor standards. Students love to engage in this activity, since it makes complex texts and concepts easier to understand because they are broken down into smaller sections to ponder.

Daily "To Own" Strategies

These daily strategies help students solve problems, debate, set goals, and focus on building self-efficacy. These four strategies will not focus solely on close reading of complex texts but will instead explore other contexts in which students can own their learning: Interactive Notebook, Walking in the Shoes of Another, Six Thinking Hats, and Socratic Seminars.

27. Interactive Notebook

An Interactive Notebook is a tool that allows students to process chunks of information during close reading of texts or other note-taking times (such as listening to a video clip or explicit instruction from teacher or peer) to achieve greater understanding and assimilation of the concept. Students process the information in deep ways prescribed by the teacher or by choice based on the daily target. The end product is an amazing, creative notebook full of the learning that students collected along the journey. This all-encompassing strategy is 21st century skills friendly, since the creativity level among the students is high, and it can accomplish almost all of the Reading and Writing anchor standards, depending on your daily target.

Preparation and Materials

Each student should have a spiral notebook or three-ring binder. Copy the Interactive Notebook reproducible (page 169 or visit **go.solution-tree.com/commoncore** to download) for each student and put it in the front of the notebook. This strategy can be ongoing throughout the school year or used for just one unit with any content (yes, even math).

One option is to use colored pencils or thin twist-up crayons. Do not use markers since they will bleed through the paper.

Instructions

Students take notes from your lesson on the right-hand side of the spiral notebook or three-ring binder in pencil, if possible. This right-hand side is the content that you want them to learn. These notes can be in any form that you choose (outline, web, or sentences), such as in figure 9.6.

After teaching, viewing a video, or reading a chunk from a book for about seven to ten minutes, stop and allow the students to process what they just learned. You can choose how they process the content, or you can give them several choices.

Once they have chosen, they will document their processing on the left-hand side of the notebook so that they can refer back to the notes. We encourage students to use colored pencils or twist-up crayons while they are writing what they processed, because certain colors enhance memory (Mehta & Zhu, 2009). This processing should be text-based, or focused on the source of the content, as much as possible to continue supporting the CCSS.

Students then continue with the next chunk of information, recording notes on the right-hand side and processing that thinking on the left-hand side. This procedure continues until the lesson is complete. Have students write or discuss a closure that summarizes all of the chunks in their notebooks.

Assessment

There are several ways to assess this strategy.

- Use the Self-Assessment and Rubric for Interactive Notebook reproducible on page 174 (or visit **go.solution-tree.com/commoncore** to download).

- Create your own expectations or criteria for success for each day's processing. How will you know students are mastering your daily targets?

Recipe Poem

Directions: Create a recipe poem for the characteristics of life. A recipe poem is set up to sound like a recipe from a cookbook, but it is for something that you couldn't use an actual recipe to make.

Think about the "ingredients" that living things need in order to be alive. You must include AT LEAST the characteristics of living things, but you may also include other ideas and vocabulary. You can start by brainstorming a list of ideas/words/phrases that could be included. An example of a format you could follow is: the title telling exactly what the recipe is for, then what ingredients are needed, how to prepare and combine them, and lastly, how to serve what you've made.

Create a rough draft on a separate sheet of paper, then NEATLY write your final draft below.

A recipe for: __Life__
- Take a handful of **cells** and combine them with two cups of **water**.
- Slowly add one cup of **proteins** and **lipids** and stir gently.
- In a separate bowl combine one half cup of **carbohydrates** and one cup **Nucleic acid** and mix
- Combine two bowls and let sit overnight. You will see the elements taking part in **respiration**, **synthesis**, and **excretion** — this is good.
- In the morning you will see the new **organism** responding to stimuli and keeping **Homeostasis** in check.
- Feel free to add a crust!

Notes for Life

Characteristics of Life:
- Cells
- Growth and development
- Reproduction
- Energy use
- Stimulus (response to surroundings)
- Common chemicals

1. Cellular Organization:
   - All living things are made up of cells
   - Bacteria are unicellular
   - Humans etc. are multicellular
2. Chemicals of Life:
   - Water is the most abundant chemical in a cell
   - Carbohydrates give energy
   - Proteins and Lipids — building materials for cells
   - Nucleic acid — generic material (DNA)
3. Energy Use
   - Energy is used for many things
   - Respiration — process of making energy from food
   - Synthesis — process of building complex molecules from simple molecules
   - Excretion — removal of waste products
4. Response to Surroundings
   - Organisms respond to stimuli in an environment
   - Internal response — homeostasis — maintenance of stable internal conditions
   - External Response

Figure 9.6: Sample Interactive Notebook.

- Have students reflect at the end of the unit by answering the questions on the Interactive Notebook: End of Unit Reflection reproducible (page 177 or visit **go.solution-tree.com /commoncore** to download).

- Use daily door passes or have students write their closure within their Interactive Notebook. Check them daily with your Cruisin' Clipboard, placing checkmarks next to their names if mastery occurred to determine who mastered the target. See the Daily Door Pass for Interactive Notebooks reproducible on page 178 (or visit **go.solution-tree.com/commoncore** to download).

We hope you will at least try Interactive Notebooks for just one unit. The Internet has many examples for all grade levels and all subject areas, and students enjoy learning from this engaging tool.

28. Walking in the Shoes of Another

Writing anchor standards one, two, eight, and nine involve students writing evidence-based arguments to support claims and examine and convey complex ideas and information clearly and accurately. Walking in the Shoes of Another (Jensen & Nickelsen, 2008) helps students appreciate and understand someone else's perspective; the goal is not necessarily to change a perspective but to respect others' perspectives. Students will then use this information to write an argument or hold a classroom debate.

Preparation and Materials

Copy one Walking in the Shoes of Another reproducible (page 179 or visit **go.solution-tree.com/common core** to download) per student. Come up with a topic in which you and someone you know have differing opinions that you can use as an example with your students. Be sure to either go over existing classroom rules or discuss how to be respectful in highly emotional situations.

Instructions

Share with your class both your perspective and a friend's perspective on a topic. Explain how you didn't necessarily agree, but you understood why that person had that perspective and respected it. Explain the importance of this attitude.

Next, ask students to help you brainstorm why appreciating other perspectives might be important in this world. What are the pros of respecting other perspectives? What are the cons of *not* respecting other perspectives? What would our world look like if we didn't appreciate or value other perspectives? What would our world look like if everyone appreciated everyone's perspectives all of the time?

Choose one of your topics that has several perspectives (politics, religion, current events, school policies, and so on). Ask students to research the topic in order to gain a perspective. Make sure they can support their perspective with well-documented facts and evidence. Students should write their perspective on the graphic organizer Walking in the Shoes of Another. Once the perspective has been thoroughly thought through and written, ask students to partner with somebody who has a different perspective.

Once partnered, they interview each other. Partner A asks the following questions, actively listening instead of writing (Jensen & Nickelsen, 2008, p. 194):

- What is your perspective on this topic?
- How can you support it?
- Where did you get this information?
- What might change your mind?

Then, Partner A takes a moment to recall what was said and ask more clarifying questions, while writing that student's perspective in the right-hand side of the table (see figure 9.7).

Now the students switch roles. Partner B asks the same four questions in order to understand Partner A's point of view on the topic.

When this interviewing and documentation stage is complete, the students take a moment to reflect on the other's perspective. They write their thoughts in the "Partner's point of view or perspective" section. At this point, students have an opportunity to change their points of view after their discussion. They should write any changes in thinking in the "The following fact or idea might change my perspective" section.

Assessment

There are a couple ways to assess this strategy.

- Use the following questions as a checklist for each student:
  - Could the student thoroughly explain his or her perspective on the issue?
  - Did the student have enough background knowledge to create the perspective?
  - Did the student support the opinion with correct details?
  - Did the student get information from a reliable resource?
  - Did the student put effort into this assignment?

- Did the student use appropriate information to explain how one could change his or her perspective?

  ▪ Create a rubric of your expectations for the writing. Ask students to help you create the criteria. Make sure there is a column for student self-assessment, peer evaluation, and teacher and parent evaluation too. It's pretty powerful to receive feedback from three other people.

You can extend this assignment by having students write a paper arguing their perspective. Feel free to use the Seven Steps for Better Argumentative Writing (see the feature box on page 146).

Research with high school students shows that debates and argumentative writing are quite engaging and exciting, especially if students have bought into their topic and are passionate about it (Yazzie-Mintz, 2010). Watch how students' emotions get highly involved during this activity.

Walking in the Shoes of Another

Topic: Injustice on Native Americans

My Name: Ty	Partner's Name: Emma
My point of view or perspective: New Americans had to fight to take America.	Partner's point of view or perspective: They had no right to take Native American land.
Why I have this perspective (support with facts): •Natives fought each other p. 222 •Other countries could take land from each other p. 249 •They signed treaties p. 225	Why do you have this perspective (support with facts)? • First people in America p. 204 •No compromise p. 215 • Didn't understand treaties p. 213
I received this information from (sources): • SS textbook •Blog: http://immigrationspot.blogspot.com /2011/03/were-native-americans-treated -fairly.html	Where did you receive your information (sources)? . http://library.thinkquest.org/J0111123/native •http://rosecity.net/tears
The following fact or idea might change my perspective: The Natives didn't understand the treaties they signed	What fact or idea could change your perspective? Natives didn't own America and countries attach each other all the time for land rights.

After the interview, put yourself in your partner's shoes. Explain what you understand, appreciate, or respect about your partner's perspective. Respond on the back of this page. After considering both perspectives, what is your perspective now? Write it on the back of this page.

I think they were treated harshly & unreasonably removed them.

Figure 9.7: Sample Walking in the Shoes of Another graphic organizer.

Seven Steps for Better Argumentative Writing

1. **Shrink your topic:** The popular topics (climate change, abortion, or freedom) are all too broad. Choose a narrower topic such as "Is climate change adversely affecting the small farmer, and if so, how?"

2. **Ensure your topic fits these three criteria:**

    a. Passion. Your topic should have emotional or cognitive *value to you*. Choose a topic you care about and are invested in.

    b. Your topic should be *currently relevant*. Does the topic matter to people right now? How?

    c. Your topic should be *arguable*. Are there people who would care enough to argue the opposite point of view?

3. **Make a plan:** Start with a few words of background on the relevancy, importance, and urgency of the topic. Then, make a claim or assertion statement and support it with evidence. You'll want three to four key points and two to three subpoints for each key point. Then summarize your claim and the support.

    You might say, "Climate change is dramatically affecting the small farmer in three ways. They are: _____."

4. **Research your topic:** Use real evidence (pictures, peer-reviewed studies, reputable unbiased journals, statistics, and case studies). Use multiple forms of evidence. Consider the smallest details as well as the big-picture view from the distance of a community, state, region, country, or the whole planet. Cite the evidence and say what case or line of thinking the evidence supports.

5. **Anticipate the other side's perspective:** Use probable scenarios to show the other point of view is unsupportable or dangerous. Show cause and effect—limit your position to specific contexts or situations so that you can be right within a context. Qualifying can not only demonstrate that you understand the complexity of an issue but can also show you have a unique perspective on it. Analyze other perspectives on your topic and prepare your defense.

6. **Conclude with a solution and summary:** Proposing a solution with a summary suggests you are an authority and makes for a strong conclusion. Here, focus on short, simple statements that restate the problem, your claim, and key evidence. Then show how your opposition points lack credibility. Finally, summarize.

7. **Test your approach:** Test your approach with another or talk it out. Check for illogical arguments and grammar mistakes. Find a peer who disagrees with your position and have him or her read your paper. Discuss your ideas, your approaches, and your writing style with this naysayer; take the feedback and advice seriously. Read your paper out loud to yourself during later revisions. Be sure to check if you've cited your sources correctly. Edit for grammar and spelling only after you are comfortable with what you've written and how you've written it. When you feel ready, you'll have a great shot at success.

29. Six Thinking Hats

This particular strategy can be used for almost all Reading, Writing, and Speaking and Listening anchor standards in the CCSS, depending on how you use it. The Six Thinking Hats comes from Edward de Bono (1999), author of *Six Thinking Hats*. This activity helps students focus on several different types of thinking one at a time in order to gain a larger perspective on a particular topic, question, or problem. Feelings, opinions, and deep perspectives will be challenged during this activity.

Preparation and Materials

Create (or have students create) six paper hats—one each in white, red, yellow, gray, green, and blue—for each group of students. Draw a top hat, football helmet, and a baseball hat template so there is a choice of which type of hat to create.

Instructions

Share with the students what the following hats mean.

- **White hat:** You brainstorm the facts that you know about _____.

- **Red hat:** You explain your feelings about _____.

- **Yellow hat:** You explain the pros or bright side of _____.

- **Gray hat:** You explain the cons or the problems that could occur with _____.

- **Green hat:** You create a "What If?" question about the topic.

- **Blue hat:** You summarize what you learned about _____.

The hats are physical symbols that trigger different kinds of thinking. When a student holds up a particular hat color, then everyone in the group must participate in that type of thinking. We recommend that students only have one hat on at a time.

There are so many benefits to using the Six Thinking Hats process in your classroom habitually. It simplifies thinking by allowing students to deal with one thought at a time, which is rare in this highly distracting world. The hats also allow students to switch their thinking or ask others to switch thinking. Finally, this strategy leads to more creative higher-level thinking. You will notice that students remain more focused and that their communication, problem-solving, and decision-making skills are enhanced.

See table 9.1 (page 148) for sentence stems that might help you and your students form better questions in each role.

There are several ways to use the hats in the classroom. For instance, the hats can help you shorten and focus meetings, solve problems, discuss topics, ask and answer questions, and experiment with ideas. Or you can even activate prior knowledge to structure the conversations students have about the topic at hand.

Students can review any content by answering questions based on the Six Thinking Hats as well. Place students in groups of six and let them choose which hat they want to represent (or you can assign particular hats to certain students depending on the needs of the learning). Whoever has the red hat responds to the red-hat question that you designed. When he or she is finished responding verbally to the whole group, the student says "open floor," at which point anybody can respond to the red-hat question. Give a time limit for each hat (blue-hat person is the timekeeper). We usually give two to three minutes per hat. There is no particular order of hats to go in—it will all depend on your purpose for using these hats—except that the blue hat

Table 9.1: Attributes and Sentence Stems for the Six Thinking Hats

HAT	ATTRIBUTES	QUESTION STEMS
White	• Facts • Information	• What do you already know about _____? • List the facts that you know about _____. • The missing facts are _____.
Red	• Feelings • Attitudes	• How do you feel about _____? • How do you think _____ felt about _____? • What is your opinion about _____? • What do you feel about doing _____?
Yellow	• Benefits • Positive thinking	• What are the benefits of _____? • What are the pros of _____? • What are the strengths of _____? • What do you like about _____? • Why will it work in order to _____?
Gray	• Judgments • Problems • Cons	• What's wrong with _____? • What potential problems could arise if _____? • Mistakes you can find are _____. • The dangers are _____. • What is bad about _____?
Green	• Creativity • New ideas • What if?	• If _____ didn't happen or did happen, _____. • What new ideas did you gather from _____? • Modifications to suggest include _____. • List the possible ways that _____. • How might you change _____? • How could you combine _____ and _____ to _____? • What new ideas do you have about improving _____?
Blue	• Summary • Organization	• What was the most valuable information that you learned from _____? • Our focus now should be _____. • What comes next is _____. • We will apply _____ by _____. • A summary of what was learned would include _____.

usually summarizes last. So, if the yellow hat is next, that student explains the benefits of the topic at hand. This continues until all hats have a chance to talk.

Try using the hats informally for small discussions such as, "I know that the hallway fight disrupted the learning, so let's take a few minutes to put on our red hats and talk about how we feel about what just happened." Or use the hats formally for tests or lessons. You can also encourage students to use the hats privately to consider thoughts about a topic or decision that needs to be made. This technique could start debates or argumentative writing as well.

Distribute the thinking questions on paper so that the students respond independently to the questions first by writing the answers down. Leave plenty of space between questions so there is room to write others' responses as well. After students answer these questions independently, pair up students and have them share their responses and add to their answers if needed.

See the following feature boxes for examples in various content area classrooms.

Assessment

There are several ways you can assess the Six Thinking Hats strategy.

- Create a checklist to determine if students formed the six thinking hat questions correctly based on your expectations and question stems in table 9.1.
- Have students evaluate one another's questions and answers.
- Encourage students to self-assess after creating their six thinking hat questions.

This strategy is sure to engage all students in different types of questions with writing, cooperative learning activities, and even classroom question design.

Insects for Primary Grades

White hat: What are some facts about insects?

Red hat: How do you feel about insects? Are there certain insects that you like to play with or be around? Are there certain insects that make you run away?

Yellow hat: What are some of the benefits of insects?

Gray hat: What are some problems that insects cause?

Green hat: What if there were not any _____?

Blue hat: What is your favorite insect, and why? Summarize what you learned about insects.

Continued →

BRINGING THE COMMON CORE TO LIFE IN K-8 CLASSROOMS

Mathematics for Third Through Fifth Grades

White hat: What are some facts about fractions?

Red hat: How do you feel about your ability to work with fractions?

Yellow hat: How do fractions benefit our world?

Gray hat: What are some problems or confusion that might occur when learning about fractions?

Green hat: What if we didn't have fractions in our world?

Blue hat: What other math concepts are related to fractions?

The Marijuana Debate for Fifth Grade

White hat: What are some facts about marijuana?

Red hat: How do you feel about marijuana being legalized in America?

Yellow hat: What would regular users of marijuana say the benefits of this drug would be? In other words, why do they take it?

Gray hat: How does marijuana affect the brain and body? What problems might occur? How does addiction happen with this drug?

Green hat: What new ideas has the medical world come up with for its use?

Blue hat: Summarize what you learned about marijuana. Do you agree with legalization of this drug—why or why not?

30. Socratic Seminars

Socratic seminars cover many of the CCSS. First, this is one of the best ways to teach and assess the Speaking and Listening standards because it is a dialogue between teacher and students and eventually between students and students. Second, students will need to know their text well in order to participate fully. They will need to annotate challenging texts in order to understand the topic in greater depths so participation happens—great critical thinking skills increase comprehension. This method is based on Socrates's theory that it is more important to enable students to think for themselves than fill their brains with content and right answers.

Preparation and Materials

Provide students with the question stems ahead of time, so they can construct while reading. Choose a text that goes along with your topic or standards. For assessment purposes, copy the Socratic Seminar Evaluation reproducible (page 180) for each student. (Visit **go.solution-tree.com/commoncore** to download all reproducibles.)

Socratic Seminar Tips

- Try to answer students' questions with questions, rather than with an answer.

- Have students number each line of the complex text that they analyzed so they can say during the discussion, "On line twelve, I noticed . . ."

- Multiple reads are encouraged with all complex texts.

- Students do not need to raise hands—model how to participate in a dialogue.

- Opinions are encouraged, but supporting opinions with text is very important.

- Small groups should be mixed by readiness levels and social skills.

- To prevent "hogs and logs" in these discussions, give each student two to three pennies that he or she will use as tokens to talk (a penny for your thoughts). When a student's pennies are gone, he or she must wait for others to use pennies before contributing more. This prevents people hogging the conversation and others from logging and not participating.

- Do not allow praising or put-downs.

- Visit the Greece Central School District website (www.greece.k12.ny.us) and search for Socratic seminars to learn more.

Instructions

Before the seminar, explain to students what a Socratic seminar looks and sounds like (use a YouTube video for your grade level). Let them know you will be guiding the first couple of seminars until you see they are ready to do this in small groups.

Share the goal with them as well: for students to participate in a dialogue wherein they each take a stand on or debate respectively about a controversial topic related to your text. This process is accomplished by engaging in conversation and asking questions so others can understand different perspectives on the topic. Go over all expectations from the evaluation sheet.

Be sure to give students plenty of time to read and annotate the chosen complex text on your topic. They will create open-ended questions that they want to discuss or want to know the answers to. You can facilitate student generation of questions by giving a few examples using the topic at hand and giving students question stems. Ideas for students to focus on during the annotation include whether they agree or disagree with the author and why, major points from the text, clarifying questions about text, why the topic is important, and so on.

During the seminar, move desks so each student can sit on the floor or in a chair within a circle. Review how students will be evaluated. Have students, in small groups of four to eight, discuss the text together with their designed questions. This could last about ten minutes. Walk around the room documenting great points the students make.

As a whole group, discuss the major points from each group. Facilitate this time with questions that you heard and ones that you created as well. Eventually, choose a student leader for this facilitation role (be sure students understand how to perform this role). This stage should take about thirty minutes.

When finished, simply say, "This is a good place to stop." Students should return the room to the original set-up and then begin evaluations. Each student should complete the Socratic Seminar Evaluation and ask another student from his or her small group to complete the peer section. This is a powerful evaluation that gets students writing about the topic too.

Assessment

There are a couple ways to assess a Socratic seminar.

- Give students these questions to ask others in the group as part of a peer evaluation:
  - Here is my view and how I arrived at it. How does it sound to you?
  - Do you see gaps in my reasoning?
  - Do you have a different interpretation? Different data?
  - Do you have different conclusions?
  - How did you arrive at your view?
  - Are you taking into account something different from what I have considered?
- Last, but not least, evaluate. See the Socratic Seminar Evaluation reproducible.

Your students will relish the opportunity to have a debate in the Socratic seminar style. We encourage you to gradually release the responsibility with this strategy. You will be amazed how quickly they will want to take on the teacher's role.

Conclusion

We hope that you will enjoy taking your students to Zone 3: Engage to Own. This level does more than connect with the Common Core; it challenges students beyond what they're used to. It is tough and requires quite a bit of reasoning skills. But ultimately, it's the most satisfying level of engagement. As students complete these activities, they'll develop a level of academic self-confidence that prepares them for far greater challenges next year.

ASQ Time

1. **Action step:** What is the single most valuable next step you will take after having read this chapter?

2. **Summary of learning:** Summarize in three to five sentences what you learned in this chapter.

3. **Question:** What discussion questions do you have for other readers, for the authors, or for self-reflection to explore more from this chapter?

Close Reading Marks

NONFICTION READING		QUESTIONS	
★	I know this already	?A	Question to author (Why did you _____?)
N	New fact or idea to me	?T	Question to teacher (Confused about text)
?	I don't understand, and here is why: _____.	?S	Question to self (Content to research)
——	Very important phrase or word to discuss	?F	Question to a friend (To review later)
☺ or ☹	I agree or disagree	WIT	What I think the answer to my question is: _____.
S	Summary time		
!	Inference I made		

FICTION READING		VOCABULARY EMPHASIS	
P	I want to predict	W	Wow Word—I like this word the author used because _____.
?	I don't understand	FL	Figurative language improved the meaning by _____.
O	What is this word?	CC	Context clue that told me the meaning of a word
✓	I get it / problem solved	△	I could change this word to _____ because _____.
C	Prediction confirmed	?A	Why did the author use this word? Predict.
!	Inference I made	?	I don't understand this word and need to look it up.
V	I visualized this		

Reciprocal Teaching Cards: Primary (Grades K–3)

THE PREDICTOR

What can I predict or conclude based on the information that I just read?

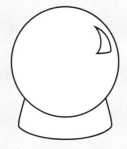

I predict that this section will be about _____ because _____ (title, subheadings, pictures, captions, tables).

Based on _____ (clue from text), I think _____.

Does anyone else have a prediction?

I think _____ because _____.

I wonder if _____ because _____.

Because I know _____ about this topic, I think _____ will be the main idea of this section.

THE SUMMARIZER

How will I summarize the pieces?

This section is mostly about _____.

The main idea of this section is _____.

Some details to support this main idea are (show from text) _____.

The author is trying to tell us _____.

Framed summary paragraph for nonfiction:

This section was mostly about _____. Some details to support it are _____, _____, _____, and _____ (show the details or pictures from the text). Let's see how the next section supports what the author is trying to convey, which is _____ (repeat main idea).

Bringing the Common Core to Life in K–8 Classrooms ©2014 Solution Tree Press • solution-tree.com
Visit **go.solution-tree.com/commoncore** to download this page.

THE QUESTIONER

What questions do we have about this text?

Who is _____?

What is/does _____?

When did _____?

Where _____?

Why did _____?

How did _____?

What is your opinion of _____? Why?

What was most important from this section? Why?

What if _____?

How are _____ and _____ similar or different?

What is an example of _____?

How would you explain _____ to _____?

Why is _____ significant?

What caused _____? What effect will occur if _____?

THE CLARIFIER

How can we make the tricky sections easy to understand?

I thought _____ was a tricky word or phrase because _____. Does anybody know what that means? What clues might tell us its meaning?

I don't understand the section _____ because _____. Can anybody explain it?

I wonder if the reader said the following word correctly because it doesn't make sense. What do you all think?

Let's reread _____, since it seems very important because _____.

I have a question about _____.

I need to look up the following word: _____.

Reciprocal Teaching Cards: Intermediate (Grades 4–8)

THE PREDICTOR

What can I predict or conclude based on this text?

Questions to Ask

What do you expect to learn from this text?

What do you think the author wants us to know and/or be able to figure out for ourselves?

What do you think is the main idea?

What might the author discuss in the next section?

What do you think would happen if _____?

What do you think caused _____ to happen?

Do you think the author is trying to teach us a lesson through this text? What is it? Why do you think that is the message the author is sending the readers in this text?

According to _____, what do you think _____ (where, how many, when)?

Phrases to Start Conversations

I think this text is going to be about _____.

The passage (or the author) suggests _____.

The author might agree _____.

I/We were correct or incorrect with our prediction because _____.

The reader might assume that _____.

Maybe it means _____.

I'm predicting that _____, and the information to support this statement is _____.

THE SUMMARIZER

How will I summarize the pieces?

Questions to Ask

What would happen if _____?

What is the key information or main idea of this text or section?

Who did what, where, when, why, and how?

What were the most important events, facts, or ideas from this reading?

How can you design, invent, compose, or arrange _____?

Can you propose alternative solutions and arrangements?

What changes would you make to solve _____?
How would you improve it?

How would you modify the plot or plan?

What could be done to minimize/maximize _____?

Can you formulate a theory for _____?

Phrases to Start Conversations

The main idea of this section is _____ (use captions, headings, pictures, and so on).

To summarize, this text is about _____.

I learned _____.

The most important information was _____.

I think the following information will be on a test about this topic: _____.

THE QUESTIONER

What questions do we have about the text?

Questions to Ask

(Ask some detailed and broader-based main idea questions; use page numbers and sections to help students go back.)

Does this photo, caption, map, diagram, or heading really reflect what we just read?

Who, what, where, when, why, how?

What if _____?

How would _____?

What do you think about _____?

THE CLARIFIER

(The questioner and clarifier sit near each other.)

How can we make the tricky sections easy to understand?

Questions to Ask

What section was confusing, and why? What should we do in order to make it less confusing?

Which words do not make sense? Are there any clues around these words?

Should we search the Internet for this phrase, time period, or concept so that we can understand this section better?

What are gaps in your thinking about _____?

This is confusing—which strategy should we choose to help us understand this better?

Phrases to Start Conversations

I don't understand the part about _____.

This doesn't make sense, so let's _____.

Oh, so you are saying _____.

Let's reread section _____.

I understand that _____ really is _____ because _____.

I agree with _____, because I now understand _____.

This word means _____ because of the following clues: _____.

Additional Reciprocal Teaching Role Cards for Grades 4–8

THE CONNECTOR

What do I already know about this topic?

Questions to Ask

Does this text remind you of anything that ever happened to you or to anyone you know? Explain.

Have you read another book that is like this one in any way? How is it the same? Different?

What do you already know about this topic that can help you understand this text better?

How is this text like something occurring in the world?

How does your connection with this text help you understand it better?

Phrases to Start Conversations

A connection I made with my life is _____.

A connection I just made about my family or friends is _____.

A connection this made me think of when I read the book or watched the movie is _____.

A connection this has to the world, my town, or family is _____.

THE ILLUSTRATOR

What clues in the illustrations or words can help me understand this reading?

Questions to Ask

What picture do you get in your mind when you read this text? Why? What words from the text told you to picture it that way?

What other senses can you access to get a good impression of the scene this text brings to your mind?

Look at pictures in the book. What did you put in your picture of this scene that the illustrator left out of his or her picture?

What other words could the author have included here to give the reader a better sense of this scene?

How did the pictures in your mind help you understand this text?

Phrases to Start Conversations

If I close my eyes, I see _____.

I see _____; I hear _____; I feel _____; I smell _____; I taste _____.

page 1 of 3

THE WONDERER

What questions will the text probably answer?

Questions to Ask

What questions has this text answered so far?

What are you still wondering about?

Why did the author write this?

Are you still confused about anything that you read? If yes, what part?

If you could ask this author a question, what would it be?

Why do you want to know this answer?

How did wondering help you understand the text better?

Phrases to Start Conversations

I think the following might happen next: _____.

I think the author will write about _____ next because _____.

I think this section will end with (solutions, ideas, and so on) _____.

I think the author's purpose for writing this section is _____.

I wonder why _____.

THE NOTICER

What clues do I notice in this text that can help me understand it?

Questions to Ask

What words in this section do you think are the most important? Why?

If you could pick only one sentence or paragraph on this page as the most important one, which would it be? Why is that one important to you?

How can you tell that the author thinks _____ is really important? Find proof in the text to support your answer.

What kind of author's craft is he or she using here to make the writing lively?

Did you notice any words within this section that might be hard to say or understand and possibly get in the way of your comprehension?

What evidence does the author use to support his or her assertions?

What is the most important idea or passage from this text? Why?

How did noticing important clues in the text help you to understand this text better?

Phrases to Start Conversations

The important clues are _____.

I guessed correctly or incorrectly about what the following clues were about: _____.

I still don't understand the following after noticing _____.

I noticed _____ because the author was so crafty when _____.

Student Steps for Reciprocal Teaching

Directions:

1. Read through your role card.

2. Create stopping points within your text by placing sticky notes on the stopping locations.

3. The stopping points indicate discussion time.

4. You will have discussions using your role cards in any order, but the following is one possible order for the discussion.

Predictor: Look through the book or text, and predict what you think the reading will be about. Use your role card to declare a statement and ask a question to your group members.

A student reads aloud the section of text up to the first stopping point.

Questioner: While reading, create some questions to ask the group. Use your role card to have statements and questions ready to go.

Clarifier: All students can contribute to what was confusing, what certain words mean, or what needs clarifying, but you are the one who leads this discussion. Be ready to share a statement and question from your role card.

Summarizer: Summarize what was just read up to the stopping point. Use your statement and questions on your role card to do this.

Predictor: Adjust your predictions and predict the next section.

Continue this process after each stopping point. Remember, this is just a suggested way to get the dialogue started, so feel free to discuss what was read in any order.

Reciprocal Teaching Conversation Notes

Names of team members and their roles: _____

Predictor: _____

Questioner: _____

Clarifier: _____

Summarizer: _____

Other Roles: _____

Text Being Read: _____

What we know:	
Our predictions:	Our questions:
Our words, phrases, or text to be clarified:	How we clarified the words, phrases, or text:
Our summary (use back of paper if necessary):	

Reciprocal Teaching Self-Assessment Form

Directions: Determine how well you worked within your group and in your role during today's reciprocal teaching time. Give yourself a rating in your assigned box and ask a peer from your group to evaluate you in his or her assigned box as well. Write explanations in the comment box.

Key: 2 = I did this often.   1 = I did this somewhat.   0 = I haven't done this yet.

ROLE	ME	PEER	COMMENTS
Predictor: _____ (name)			
I predicted before we read each section.			
I asked others if they agreed with my prediction and asked why or why not?			
I previewed the text by looking at titles, pictures, tables, captions, subheadings, and so on.			
Each prediction was supported by evidence from text.			
I listened and respected others' comments in my group.			
Questioner: _____ (name)			
I created higher-level questions that required others to infer.			
I gave my answers to my questions after others contributed.			
I reworded my questions when students were stuck.			

page 1 of 3

My questions focused on the main idea of the text.			
I listened and respected others' comments in my group.			

Clarifier: _____ (name)

During each section, I wrote down unknown words, tricky sections, unique phrases, and reading strategies that were used to discuss at the stopping point.			
I encouraged the group to use powerful reading strategies to help us understand tricky sections of the text.			
I looked up meanings to words to share with the group.			
I asked the teacher questions if we couldn't figure out a tricky section.			
I listened and respected others' comments in my group.			

Summarizer: _____ (name)

I summarized each section thoroughly by focusing on the main idea of the section.			
I gave important, text-based details to support the main idea that I used in my summary.			
I asked others to contribute to my summaries.			
I listened and respected others' comments in my group.			

page 2 of 3

Overall group strengths:

Overall group improvements:

We learned the following information from our reading:

We still have the following questions from our reading:

Bringing the Common Core to Life in K–8 Classrooms ©2014 Solution Tree Press • solution-tree.com
Visit **go.solution-tree.com/commoncore** to download this page.

Stop-n-Think With Checkpoints

Box 1 (warm-up):	☐ Got It ☐ Need More Practice ☐ Not Yet
Box 2:	☐ Got It ☐ Need More Practice ☐ Not Yet
Box 3:	☐ Got It ☐ Need More Practice ☐ Not Yet
Box 4:	☐ Got It ☐ Need More Practice ☐ Not Yet
Box 5 (closure):	☐ Got It ☐ Need More Practice ☐ Not Yet

Stop-n-Think for Primary Students

Topic or Book: _____

Box 1: Beginning

Box 2: Middle

Box 3: End

Interactive Notebook

This style of notebook uses both the right and left hemispheres of the brain to help sort, categorize, and be creative with the newly attained knowledge. The right side of the notebook is for writing down information given by the teacher (notes, vocabulary, video notes, labs, and so on). The left side is for documenting your understanding of the information (brainstorming, reflections, drawings, figures, and so on).

What Are These Notebooks?

- A tool that allows you to be creative, independent thinkers and writers
- An organizer for questions, what was learned, summaries, and so on
- A tool for processing what was learned through various modalities (writing, drawing, webbing, discussion, and so on) and critical thinking activities
- A place to make learning a rough draft and highly engaging
- A formative assessment tool for teachers to see where you are with the standards

What Supplies Do You Need?

- Colored pencils (no markers)
- Pens and pencils
- Glue stick
- Three-ring binder or notebook

How Do You Organize the Notebook?

Decorate the cover page with the unit topic, your name, subject area, and dates of use. Include a table of contents explaining the pages where the content is located (number all pages after the table of contents). The end of the notebook should include the following sections so you have these ideas for processing always within your notebook.

What Do You Do on the Right Side?

Content being learned goes on the right side of the notebook, including information from teachers, books, computers, articles, and so on. Use pencil. Following is a list of the type of information to include on the right side.

- Title or heading of the topic
- Glued or stapled complex texts
- Date of the notes being taken
- Source the content comes from (science book, website, video, and so on)
- Information written down as it is given in class
- Notes from books, videos, readings, the Internet, and so on

- Cornell Notes
- Special notes from teacher—use cloze note-taking to fill in blanks during the minilesson
- Vocabulary words and their definitions
- Notes about labs, lab instructions, procedures, and materials
- Teacher questions
- Sample math problems

What Do You Do on the Left Side?

Student thinking about and understanding of the information from the right side is then documented on the left side of the notebook. This is the processing side—it shows what is going on in *your* brain after learning what is documented on the right. Left-side pages are a place to interact with content from the right side in creative, unique, and individual ways. Use colored pencils and regular pencil. Color enhances memory.

Following is a list of the type of information to include on the left side.

- Brainstorming ideas, webs, concept maps, and mindmaps
- Illustrations, pictures, or images from the Internet glued (glue sticks only since bottled glue soaks through the paper; students will be gluing many templates into the notebook)
- Venn diagrams or H diagrams
- Other graphic organizers
- Data and graphs from labs
- Diagrams, charts, tables, or flowcharts that you create
- Answers to questions from the right side of the notebook
- Questions that your peers generate and then answer
- Simile summaries
- Quick writes
- Poetry, raps, songs, creative writing, and acrostic poems
- Writing prompts
- Observations of demonstrations
- Comic strip
- Hypothesis development
- Survey, Question, Read, Write, Recite, and Review (SQ4R) and other reading responses
- Summaries with one sentence or phrase
- Small-group activity responses

What If You Need Help With the Left Side?

This section contains various ways to help you jumpstart your processing.

Sentence Stems to Get You Started

- A summary of what I learned is _____.
- The most important things to understand about _____ are _____.
- This concept is related to _____ because _____.
- Remember to _____ when solving this math problem _____.
- The main idea of _____ is _____.
- The word _____ means _____.
- One event from my reading to elaborate on is _____.
- An illustration of what I learned or visualized while reading looks like _____.
- A way to solve _____ is _____.
- An example of how one event from the reading supports our theme of _____ is _____.
- I'm beginning to wonder _____ now that I have learned _____.
- Some examples of _____ are _____.
- In my opinion, _____.
- I believe _____ is beneficial/harmful/dangerous because _____.
- I think _____ is necessary/unimportant because _____.
- I feel _____ is important because _____.
- I used to feel/believe _____, but now I feel/believe _____ because _____.
- Here is a possible way to solve the following problem: _____.
- Some details that I learned today are _____.
- Some questions that should help me understand _____ better are _____.
- I made a personal connection with _____ because _____.

Ten Prompts for the Left Side

1. What was I curious about in today's learning? What would I like to test/do next?
2. What was the main idea and important details to support it?
3. What do I need to understand better?
4. What can I create to help me remember what I just learned?
5. How can I improve my home, school, community, country, or world after learning this information?
6. Create a "What If?" question and answer it.
7. Write a letter to a friend or younger student explaining what you learned.

8. Create a simile, metaphor, or analogy about what you learned.

9. Write problems about the topic and solve them.

10. How did this information personally connect with you?

Just-Right Questions

Generate a question from the following choices and then answer the question on the left side of your notebook. Take one word from the Choice A column and combine it with one word from the Choice B column to form the perfect question stem.

CHOICE A	CHOICE B
Who	Is
What	Did
Where	Can
When	Would
Why	Will

Ways to Process Vocabulary Words

- Give an example of the word.

- Give a nonexample of the word.

- Create a question about the word.

- Create a simile or metaphor using the word.

- Use the word in a different way from the original text.

- Give synonyms for the word.

- Give antonyms for the word.

- Create a short story with classmates using the word.

- Draw a quick picture or symbol of the word.

- Explain how the word relates to your life.

- Give additional information or more facts about the word.

- Paraphrase what the word means.

- Create a different sentence for the word.

- Explain how this word relates to the world currently.

How Do You Use This Notebook to Study?

1. Review your notes every night, and summarize your learning on the left side.

2. Teach the content to your family.

3. Mindmap the whole unit before the test to see the connections and the bigger pictures.

4. Document all of the vocabulary words by placing them on index cards. Quiz yourself.

5. Create a test using the information in your Interactive Notebook.

6. After the test, staple it to the right side and then, on the left side, reflect on why you missed certain questions. Use this format: list the question number, write the correct answer, redo or resolve, and explain why you missed it.

7. Highlight the most important information or information that you still don't know well with a yellow crayon, pencil, or small sticky notes.

8. Create questions using the content from the right side. Write these questions on index cards and then write the answer on the opposite side. Test yourself!

Parent-Student Communication Log

Dear parents,

This page will allow your child to learn content for the long term. When one person teaches another, the information has another opportunity to be rehearsed and more strongly connected to other content. In other words, the student who teaches content learns it better! Let your child teach you what he or she learned.

Once a week, have your child explain the most valuable information he or she learned from this Interactive Notebook. Please make sure he or she elaborates and doesn't just list facts. The more questions you ask, the more your child will learn. Then fill out the following chart.

DATE	WHAT PARENT LEARNED	PARENT SIGNATURE

Bringing the Common Core to Life in K–8 Classrooms ©2014 Solution Tree Press • solution-tree.com
Visit **go.solution-tree.com/commoncore** to download this page.

Self-Assessment and Rubric for Interactive Notebook

Directions: Please use the Self-Evaluation column to give yourself a score for notebook organization, classwork, processing, and notebook visuals. The teacher will evaluate your notebook on the far right-hand side column after your evaluation.

Unit: _____

CATEGORY	4	3	2	1	SELF-EVALUATION	TEACHER EVALUATION
Notebook Organization	All pages have numbers, titles, dates, and self-evaluations. Table of contents goes along with page numbers. Pages are neat and organized.	Notebook is missing a few page numbers, titles, dates, and self-evaluations. Table of contents matches up somewhat. Pages are fairly neat and organized.	Notebook is missing many page numbers, titles, dates, and self-evaluations. Table of contents doesn't match up well with pages. Pages are fairly neat and organized.	Notebook is missing most page numbers, titles, dates, and self-evaluations. Table of contents is missing. Notebook is not neat or organized.		
Classwork (right side—input)	All notes are present. Notes are neat, detailed, and accurate.	Most notes are present. Notes are fairly neat, detailed, and accurate.	Very few notes are present. Notes are not very neat, detailed, or accurate.	Most notes are not present. Notes are not neat, detailed, or accurate.		

CATEGORY	4	3	2	1	SELF-EVALUATION	TEACHER EVALUATION
Processing (left side—output)	Output is present for all work. Output is detailed, creative, and rigorous (effort to be challenged) and shows great understanding of content on right. Extra effort is shown.	Output is present for most work. Output has some detail, creativity, and rigor, and some understanding is shown. Effort is shown.	Output is missing on several pages or is incomplete. Output has a little detail, creativity, or rigor, and it shows a little understanding. Little effort is shown.	Output is missing on almost all pages. Output is not creative, detailed, or rigorous. Student shows no understanding of outcome. No effort is shown.		
Notebook Visuals	Visuals are creative. There are at least two visuals per output page. Visuals are colorful and purposeful.	Visuals are somewhat creative. There are one to two visuals per output page. Visuals are somewhat colorful and purposeful.	Little creativity is shown. There is only one visual on the output page. Visual has little color, and the purpose is not clear.	No creativity is expressed. There are no visuals, color, or purpose.		

CATEGORY	4	3	2	1	SELF-EVALUATION	TEACHER EVALUATION
Other:						

Total Points

Strengths:

Growth Opportunities:

Interactive Notebook: End of Unit Reflection

1. What was your most valuable piece of information of this unit, and why?

2. What left-side entries do you believe were the highest quality, and why?

3. What activities during this unit impacted you the most? The least? Why?

4. What would you do differently after evaluating your Interactive Notebook for this unit?

5. What new ideas do you have for the next unit's Interactive Notebook?

Bringing the Common Core to Life in K–8 Classrooms ©2014 Solution Tree Press • solution-tree.com
Visit **go.solution-tree.com/commoncore** to download this page.

Daily Door Pass for Interactive Notebooks

Copy, cut apart, and have these door passes ready for students to glue into their notebooks three minutes before the subject area or class ends. Students place open notebooks in a pile by the door so the teacher can quickly glance at the door pass results. Write the daily target required for your lesson in the appropriate box, and have students check the appropriate box if they got it, sort of got it, or have not yet gotten it. Ask students to then complete the demonstration or explanation. This pass is the proof or evidence that they did get the target. If it is multiplying two fractions together, they must show they can do that in the demonstration box. If the target is to analyze what caused World War I, then they will list causes and give evidence from the text in this box. You will check each of these door passes to determine who needs additional teaching and support.

Self-Evaluation			Daily Target
☐ I Got It!	☐ I Sort of Got It!	☐ I Haven't Gotten It Yet!	Target: _____ Date: _____
Demonstrate or Explain:			

Self-Evaluation			Daily Target
☐ I Got It!	☐ I Sort of Got It!	☐ I Haven't Gotten It Yet!	Target: _____ Date: _____
Demonstrate or Explain:			

Self-Evaluation			Daily Target
☐ I Got It!	☐ I Sort of Got It!	☐ I Haven't Gotten It Yet!	Target: _____ Date: _____
Demonstrate or Explain:			

Walking in the Shoes of Another

Topic: _____

My Name:	Partner's Name:
My point of view or perspective:	Partner's point of view or perspective:
Why I have this perspective (support with facts):	Why do you have this perspective (support with facts)?
I received this information from (sources):	Where did you receive your information (sources)?
The following fact or idea might change my perspective:	What fact or idea could change your perspective?

After the interview, put yourself in your partner's shoes. Explain what you understand, appreciate, or respect about your partner's perspective. Respond on the back of this page. After considering both perspectives, what is your perspective now? Write it on the back of this page.

Socratic Seminar Evaluation

Name of Student: _____   Topic Discussed: _____

3 = Went above and beyond the expectations   1 = Could have improved because . . .

2 = Did what was expected   0 = No evidence at all

CRITERIA	STUDENT	PEER	TEACHER	EXPLAIN
Participant paraphrased others' comments before agreeing or disagreeing.				
Participant demonstrated a deep knowledge of the text, class notes, and the topic. Participant offered solid evidence for his or her perspectives.				
Participant asked appropriate, open-ended questions. Participant responded to others' questions with a question.				
Participant came to the seminar prepared with notes and a marked and annotated text.				
Participant showed that he or she was actively listening to other participants (looked speaker in the eyes, used names, used respectful tone, and didn't interrupt).				
Participant offered clarification or follow-up that extended the conversation.				
Participant's remarks often referred back to specific parts of the text.				

1. Explain how you prepared for this Socratic seminar.

2. What could you have been more prepared for during the discussion, and what plan can you create to know that topic or subtopic better?

3. After reflecting on what others contributed to the seminar, whose contribution was most helpful to you? Why?

4. Write about your new thoughts and ideas regarding the passage and the discussions.

Bringing the Common Core to Life in K–8 Classrooms ©2014 Solution Tree Press • solution-tree.com
Visit **go.solution-tree.com/commoncore** to download this page.

CHAPTER 10

THE BIG PICTURE

With all good daily targets comes careful thought about the big picture. We want to simplify the process for those who want the overall view of creating a cognitively engaging unit. We believe the following template will help you challenge students at all thinking levels and zones.

We start with a Unit Plan Organizer to help you create a map for a unit. Then we look at a one-page lesson plan template for lessons lasting one to three days. Following that, we discuss the role of formative assessment throughout a unit in conjunction with ideas for differentiating your instruction based on the outcomes of those formative assessments. Finally, we close with advice on transformative habits, how staff development can better support strategy implementation, and self-empowerment.

Unit Plan Organizer

The Unit Plan Organizer will help you map out an engaging unit. The first section of the organizer is all about the basic details and the standards (see figure 10.1). It covers the subject that you're teaching (English, mathematics, social studies); grade level (first, fifth, twelfth); unit of study (geology, fractions, westward movement); length of unit (how many days); dates the unit will begin and end; and essential questions of the unit (see the Klamath Falls City Schools [n.d.] essential questions guide; visit **go.solution-tree.com /commoncore** for a live link). The biggest box in this first section is where you list the standards that will be covered in this unit.

Subject:	Grade level:	Unit of study:
Approximate length of unit: Number of days to reteach or enrich: Dates:		Essential questions of unit:
Standards covered in this unit (CCSS ELA and essential standards in your content area):		

Figure 10.1: Section 1 of the Unit Plan Organizer.

The next section of the organizer looks a little deeper and may take longer to fill out than section 1 (see figure 10.2). The first box is for concepts or themes students will learn in the unit. The second box is where you list the skills students will be able to do (mindmap, analyze, sort, compare/contrast, and other engaging verbs). The third box is fun—brainstorm a list of engaging activities or tasks that the students might participate in during this unit (this doesn't have to be perfect, just ideas). Then, take the vocabulary words that need to be taught and organize them around the concepts or categories listed earlier. This web can be used throughout the unit as a word wall. Finally, in the last box, list the resources, materials, technology, websites, or complex texts that will be used throughout the unit.

Concepts students will learn (what they need to know):	Skills students need to be able to do:
Engaging activities, tasks, or learning experiences students will engage in (projects, graphic organizers, group simulations, research, plays, and presentations):	
Vocabulary web of words learned during this unit (can use back of page):	
Resources, materials, technology, or texts:	

Figure 10.2: Section 2 of the Unit Plan Organizer.

This Unit Plan Organizer is the first step toward daily lesson plan success. For a reproducible version, see page 193 or visit **go.solution-tree.com/commoncore** to download.

Now, let's go a step deeper into the unit and explore the one-page lesson plan for lessons that are one to three days long. These lessons are specific and measurable.

Engaging Lesson Plan Template

Now that you have the big picture in mind, it's time to start planning the daily lessons. This stage breaks down the larger unit into individual lesson plans that connect the various standard-based targets we learned how to create in chapter 3. We like to create our lesson plans with other teachers so that the ideas flow quickly and powerfully. One person types while the others brainstorm. We keep these awesome lesson plans together in a large file folder so that we can use them in the future, with some tweaks, of course, since we have learned what does and does not work, and we have different students. After teaching the lessons, make sure to document any changes you want to make the next year.

To begin this process, take your standards from the Unit Plan Organizer and break that big picture into smaller lessons of achievable skills or information. You might have a science standard combined with a Common Core ELA standard so that there are reading and writing components too. Integration will be a must with the CCSS.

On a scrap piece of paper, list the four to six targets that will help your students reach those standards. Then sequence them to determine individual lessons; some targets may take one to three days to accomplish. Robyn Jackson's (2011) book *How to Plan Rigorous Instruction* explains how to unpack standards. Grant Wiggins and

Jay McTighe (2005) also give a tremendous amount of detail in how to create a unit plan in *Understanding by Design*.

Using the Engaging Lesson Plan Template reproducible (page 194), write the three-step power target—Do, Know, Show—in the target box. Remember, the Do is the verb (how the students will be thinking), the Know is the specific content they will need to know or perform, and the Show is the product or the evidence of learning that tells you if the student accomplished the target.

Under that target, list what engagement zone the target falls into—Engage to Build Basics, Engage to Explore, or Engage to Own (see table 3.1, page 33). You will know by its verb. You might even be planning this lesson within two zones; it's fine to have more than one of the engagement zones represented in a lesson. The goal is at least one zone per lesson to ensure engagement and higher levels of thinking. We plan many lessons with a Zone 1 strategy to activate prior knowledge and a Zone 2 or 3 strategy for the main part of the lesson. Be sure to determine which materials, texts, or technology pieces you will need for this daily lesson.

Finally, check the criteria for success. Decide on an assessment and plan to share what is expected from the students during the lesson. Will you provide a rubric, checklist, exemplar, conference with small groups or individual students, peer or self-evaluations, or observations? It's extremely important that the students know exactly what the target and expectations are for success with this lesson.

Now it's time for the second section of the lesson plan. What activities or tasks will students engage in to get to the target? Just keep in mind that everything you place in your lesson plan must help the students achieve the target (see figure 10.3).

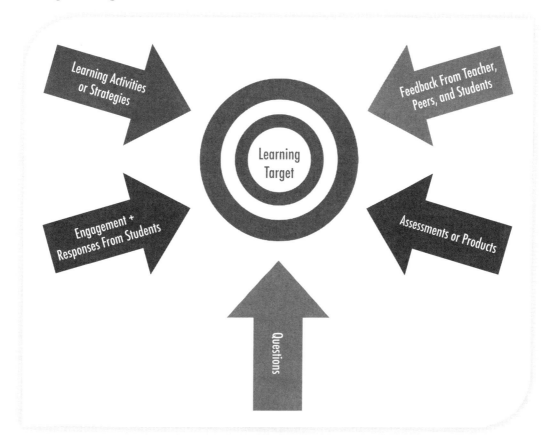

Figure 10.3: Using everything in a lesson helps students reach the target.

Some teachers call this section the agenda. We tend to list lesson activities on a dry-erase board. It might look like this: writing prompt, Super Sleuth, Close Reading Marks, and door pass. Then we place the agenda items right next to the target (Do, Know, Show). We write the Do and the Know on the board for the students. The students receive the Show as the assignment. We must tell our students the target and agenda so they know exactly where they are with the learning target, which gets them to the big standard. At this point, use the checklist on the right side of the reproducible to check off which engagement strategies you will be using during this lesson. This is simply a quick check to keep our minds focused while creating our daily lesson plan.

Next, think about what you know about your students so you can plan how you might need to differentiate for them. We have a whole list of differentiation options in appendix A (page 197). In addition, study the large vocabulary web that you created in the Unit Plan Organizer along with the readings planned, and determine which words should be taught with this particular target. Place these words in the vocabulary box on the Engaging Lesson Plan Template reproducible.

Now, create higher-level questions to ask your students during this lesson. When we plan questions in advance versus in the spur of the moment, we create more higher-level thinking questions and questions that are more congruent with our target. Raising the rigor within all of our lessons will be very important to get our students to CCSS mastery. We also want to encourage students to create their own questions. You can find question stems for your engagement zone on the following pages: Zone 1, page 51; Zone 2, page 90; Zone 3, page 121.

Last but certainly not least is deciding how you will know if the students are getting to the target. This step is one of the most important. In fact, it is so important that we are going to elaborate on how to formatively assess your students within each daily lesson.

The Formative Assessment Process

Every strategy to enhance the engagement zones in this book is a type of formative assessment to see if students are getting close to your target. The only way a formative assessment process is powerful and useful is if you either give feedback to your students to help them determine how to reach the target or you change your instruction based on what you observe.

The formative assessment process can be easily summarized with the Cha-Cha-Chas: Chunk, Chew, Check, and Change. Melissa Dickson, a well-known educational consultant, and LeAnn wrote a song to explain to teachers in the Anne Arundel County Public Schools in Maryland just how easy the formative assessment process is to implement in every classroom. (We actually do a little dance with it too.) It goes like this:

> Chunk it, we teach a bit
>
> Chew it, they think about it
>
> Check it, do they know?
>
> Change it, to watch them grow

The Cha-Cha-Chas will ensure mastery of the daily target. Doing all these steps will double the speed of learning. Really? Double? Yes! When implemented well, the formative assessment process can effectively double the speed of student learning (Wiliam, 2007). Dylan Wiliam's research is a synthesis of more than four thousand research studies in the last forty years. This research focuses on feedback that was given minutes, hours, or days rather than weeks or months later. In addition, Paul Black and Wiliam (1998a) conducted an extensive research review of 250 journal articles and book chapters narrowed from a much larger pool to determine whether formative assessment raises academic standards in the classroom. They concluded that the formative assessment process produces significant learning gains. Effect sizes ranged between 0.40 and 0.70, with formative assessment apparently helping low-achieving students, including students with special needs, even more than it helped other students (Black & Wiliam, 1998b).

The steps are as follows.

1. Provide a clear and understandable vision of the learning target each day (say it, show it, and go over it throughout the lesson). Students should be able to explain what is expected of them that day. First, students acquire a small *chunk* of information (of course, in a differentiated way). This could be from a short video clip, your minilesson, reading, the Internet, a webquest, software programs, each other, centers, and so on.

2. Students then *chew* the chunk just learned. Choose a way (or let them choose) for the students to chew or think about the content. The important part is what the kids *do* with what they just learned: create a web or graph, sort, act out, annotate, analyze, synthesize, research, and so on. To explain the chew step, use examples of strong and weak work. Make sure it's extremely clear what is expected from them. This can be done by providing checklists, rubrics, written explanations, and examples galore, otherwise known as criteria for success.

3. Offer regular descriptive feedback while they chew. This is the *check* for understanding about where they are in relationship to that target. Teach students to self-assess their learning and set goals based on their needs. You should also design a way to assess the students' level of understanding of what was taught (break this into several components). For instance, you might need to focus on each quality within the rubric and fully explain what each quality looks like.

4. Let students practice what they learned, and revise according to feedback from a rubric, self, others, and the teacher; this might be a time for you to reteach or even enrich. This process is the *change* section of the Cha-Cha-Chas, and daily data are needed to perform this last step. You must change your instruction based on what the students need. This is the powerful part of differentiation.

Make sure all four sections of the formative assessment process are present in daily lessons so that you can double the speed of learning. Close the class by asking students to reflect on that day's lesson (target question, important learning, goal for tomorrow, and so on). Closures are important to the learning process because:

- Students summarize their learning based on the learning target that day

- They improve memory of concepts taught during that lesson

- They keep students more engaged since they will know they will be held accountable

- They provide data to help you change instruction that day or the next

Another great opportunity to check for understanding is by collecting door passes—now you have proof of how close students are to the target. These passes can be used to change your instruction for the next day if need be. Door passes allow students to quickly respond to a prompt from you after the lesson. This prompt is *always* about the target. With the CCSS, we will need to know where students are with the standards daily. Students will need to check for their own understanding and have evidence of learning. Door passes give you and the student evidence of where he or she is with that day's learning target.

The Door Passes reproducible (page 195 or visit **go.solution-tree.com/commoncore** to download) has four passes. Cut them apart and give each student one. Have many of these door passes ready to go, since closure needs to be a part of every lesson. Door passes are excellent, quick ways for students to respond to that day's lesson and demonstrate comprehension. And, being at the door and wishing students well as they exit is a very positive way to end the period or subject. The door pass is one of our favorite tools for the formative assessment process; we've learned that it keeps students more engaged during the lesson, since they will be held accountable for thinking one last time at the end of the lesson.

Ways to Differentiate Instruction

Once you have the results from your formative assessments, you'll know what needs to change in your future instruction. When some students struggle or others have mastered the concept, we shouldn't reteach the whole class. Instead, consider the following options for students who got it, students who need more practice, and students who did *not* get it.

For those who got it, try anchor activities: a highly engaging and somewhat challenging activity embedded into the current curriculum that students independently complete while other students need you to reteach or explain differently. One of our favorite anchor activities is when a student has a question and wants to research it independently and share it in his or her own special way. Students love to answer real questions that come up while learning and yet are not part of the regular curriculum. You can also extend the learning, go deeper with their interests in this area of curriculum, or compact the curriculum (visit www.gifted.uconn.edu to learn more about curriculum compacting; visit **go.solution-tree.com /commoncore** for a live link).

For those who need more practice, provide a variety of examples, define words in elaborative ways, teach in smaller chunks and check their processing of what they just learned, and have them teach someone else to check for understanding. We like to place these kids with someone who got it and play a game called Coach and Player. The coach tells the player how to do the target skill step by step, and the player must do each step accordingly. Then, they switch roles so the new coach tells the new player how to do the skill. It's important that the student who got it is the coach first.

For those who did *not* get it, reteach at a table using manipulatives, images, and graphic organizers; teach a small chunk and check for understanding often; and give them more practice. Make sure they can do this skill on their own after reteaching, watch their facial expressions, and keep the group small so you can read your students. For more ways to change instruction, see appendix A (page 197), which is a differentiation cheat sheet for planning engaging lessons.

You now have a Unit Plan Organizer (page 193) and an Engaging Lesson Plan Template (page 194) that will help you pull all the pieces together from this book. When we plan with engagement, CCSS, and differentiation in mind, we plan on having many students successfully reaching the target and wanting to experience learning more.

Transformative Habits

You may be saying, "I have many of these healthy, powerful teaching habits going on daily in my classroom, but I'm still missing some." Maybe you want to make closures a habit in your classroom. Maybe you want to respond to daily data in your classroom and find time to change your instruction to meet the needs of your students. Habits can and do change, but how?

Habits are made up of three steps—(1) the cue, (2) the routine, and (3) the reward (see figure 10.4).

Figure 10.4: The three steps of habits.

Let's use these three steps to create a habit—for instance, doing closures every day in the classroom. *Cue* could be your time-conscious student Katie waving her hands in the air three minutes before the bell rings. (Ask a student to volunteer for this role—he or she can't wait to interrupt you!) This cue tells you and your students it's time to stop everything and fill out a door pass (already at each student's desk because it was a *routine* to pick one up when he or she entered the classroom). On their way out of the classroom, they place their door pass in the red, yellow, or green file folder that is taped strongly to the wall. Red means they didn't understand the lesson and didn't get to the target yet, yellow means they are getting close but need more practice, and green means they understood the lesson well and reached the target. The *reward* is that they get to leave the classroom and see their peers in the hallway, or maybe it's a high five from you on the way out. The reward could also be extra help the next day if they were in the red or yellow zone. Keep rewards to a minimum on this task (Deci, Koestner, & Ryan, 1999), though rewards theoretically might include privileges like being first at something, getting to use certain new technology, playing or downloading a favorite song, and so on.

What habits did you learn about in this book that you would like to instill in your daily classroom routines? Tell another teacher about them, read about them, understand them well, and then use the three steps to create powerful teaching habits that will make your job easier and students' learning more successful. To learn more about habits, read *The Power of Habit* by Charles Duhigg (2012).

Support of Strategy Implementation

There are two types of support for implementation: schoolwide and personal. Both are important. If you currently play a role in staff development—if you're an administrator, instructional coach, or a lead teacher who shares your work with others—this next section is for you. When teachers feel supported, they're more likely to carry out the changes needed to support student achievement. Making these changes once is a great start; turning them into habits is priceless.

Here are our top five ways to support implementation.

1. **Instructional coaching:** Coaching is the use of a savvy trainer or teacher mentor who can work with teachers in their classroom to influence teacher quality. If you can secure coaching for yourself, embrace it. If it is not provided, set up situations where you can observe another teacher (by video or in person) and get or give feedback using these strategies. This provides handholding with feedback and error correction for better quality of implementation. Coaching can be the vehicle for developing great habits.

2. **Building the staff learning culture:** Encourage a culture of implementation and feedback that says, "We, as a school, expect staff to be lifelong learners, and our professional development is partly the responsibility of the school and partly the responsibility of the staff." A culture of constant learning is often referred to as the *growth mindset*, which moves progress ahead quickly. When teachers promote this climate and use the opportunities to learn and refine the practices proposed by the change agents, change is accelerated (Cohen & Hill, 2001).

3. **Collaboration:** This technique will make your job easier! Work with grade-level content teams to target specific strategies from this book. Teams alone won't make the magic of implementation happen; they're simply the raw material for a vehicle of change. But we know that without teams, the odds of success are lower. Teachers in teams or, on a bigger scale, who are part of a professional learning community have a better understanding of how to implement the professional development experiences on content, which is critical (Birman, Desimone, Garet, & Porter, 2000).

4. **Administrative support over time:** Be sure to have your staff's back as they begin to implement. While quick progress creates excitement and momentum, evidence suggests that instructional change is more effective when there's enough time invested by staff to understand, integrate, and fine-tune the changes. Without this time, the degree of implementation drops. The key ingredient is that the learning is fostered over time, which is what the evidence tells us works best. Several studies indicate that professional development should be continuous, not episodic, and should include follow-up and support for further learning (Association for Supervision and Curriculum Development, 2003).

5. **Maximum alignment:** Tie together instruction with curriculum and assessment. This book is already designed to help you do that. When this alignment happens, you'll see quicker results, since the work is better tied to classroom results. You're more likely to implement work that fits with the curriculum and will show up on the assessment you're already using instead of something brand new (Baker & Smith, 1999).

Self-Empowerment

Even if you're not getting massive support, several factors have emerged as being powerful allies for your own individual support. Yes, you can take responsibility for, and revel in the success of, implementing the strategies in this book in your work. We have chosen five factors that will help you become more self-empowered. Becoming a master teacher is as much about planning thoughtful strategies as super creativity or a daily force of will. Here is how you can support your own habits of success.

1. **Reflect:** Evidence suggests that a reflective staff is more likely to think through the proposed adjustment, evaluate it, and better implement the change (Dutro, Fisk, Koch, Roop, & Wixson, 2002). The days of, "Ready, fire, and aim!" are gone. Here's the reflection process in the form of questions for you or a colleague to answer as you implement the strategies—

    • Do you know the intended result of this activity or process? Does this build clarity, understanding, memory, pre-knowledge, or student achievement?

    • Do you have a clear idea of how to implement this step by step? If not, let's chunk it down into smaller steps and think it through.

    • Do you have ways to alter, deviate from, tweak, or escape this if we are interrupted or if it's not working at all? If not, take a moment and write down your contingency plan.

- Once you have used the strategy, what worked, and what could work better next time? Write these down, so you'll remember them.

- Do you have a system for keeping track of your teaching, so you can correct mistakes and get better each time? If not, buy a journal or open up a digital file for this.

2. **Achieve quick, measured, relevant gains:** If you want quick progress, choose a crucial behavior that gives you a high return on it when done well. Look over the strategies carefully, and pick one that can clearly help you get the outcome you want. Make a quick plan for how you'll use it and what your personal criteria for success are.

3. **Get your carrot and stick going:** Find the values, mission, or drivers that move you forward. When our goals are tied to what motivates and drives us, they are more likely to happen. Continually remember what moves you ahead. Is it any of these?

   - Autonomy

   - Mastery

   - Sense of purpose

   - Bonding with friends

   - Learning something new

   - Social fun (teams and learning communities)

   - Pleasure with teaching as a career and helping kids succeed

   We also suggest you go to the website www.stickk.com and list your main goal. Set up your customized carrot and stick to encourage you to become the best teacher you can be.

4. **Focus on perfect practice:** We've all heard that practice does not make perfect, it makes permanent. But what kind of practice helps teachers (or anyone) learn a skill in ways that they get to the right or perfect skill level quickly and stay there? It's known as perfect practice. This type of practice was pioneered by K. Anders Ericsson, the Swedish psychologist and Conradi Eminent Scholar at Florida State University, who is widely recognized as the world's leading expert on the acquisition of expert performance and deliberate practice. He determined that those at the absolute top of their field did indeed practice differently than the rest. They (1) chose what to practice very carefully, (2) got feedback from a coach (or mirror), (3) made immediate corrections, and (4) practiced until they got it perfect (Ericsson, Krampe, & Tesch-Romer, 1993). This type of practice rarely ever happens, but you can be the exception.

5. **Create your nudges:** While many think that what prompts us to make changes in our life is our skill or willpower, a line of new research is suggesting it may be much simpler (Thaler & Sunstein, 2008). Sometimes a well-placed iPad reminder, a note, or poster in the back of the classroom can be all it takes to implement the activity. Where do you place your nudges? Let's follow the cookie crumbs from your learning to the classroom. Here are just some of the potential gaps.

   - Where is the actual strategy you want to use? Identify the location. If it's in this book only, *nudge it*! Transfer it to an email, index card, notebook, iPad, mindmap, or notepad.

   - Once it's on a second medium (other than this book), where will you put the strategy? *Nudge it!* Set up a prompt in the classroom to use it. Embed it in the lesson plan or post it.

- Once you've used it, what's your plan for debriefing and improving it? Before you use it, send yourself a *nudge*! Send yourself a follow-up email to arrive the next day. Visit www.futureme .org so that you have a future email prompt waiting for you. This is your own form of support, even if there's not an effective professional learning community in place.

Conclusion

You can successfully implement one of the book's strategies every two weeks. It takes time to understand, plan, and debrief each one, and you'll want to give yourself some written feedback so you can do it better next time. Use the strategy again, and implement your corrections. Over the length of a school year, that's going to be ten to fifteen strategies at most. If you feel more comfortable with fewer, use half that number, but the routine is the same: plan, implement, debrief, make corrections, and prep for next time. This is the path to mastery. Mastery is the only real game there is in teaching. It gives you all the goodies: improved student achievement, lower stress in the classroom, fewer misbehaviors, admiration by your peers, and career opportunities.

When you instill these smarter teaching habits and implementation changes, the CCSS are more achievable, the joy-factor improves among students and staff, engagement levels rise, and teaching gets easier because success is in the air.

ASQ Time

1. **Action step:** What is the single most valuable next step you will take after having read this chapter?

2. **Summary of learning:** Summarize in three to five sentences what you learned in this chapter.

3. **Question:** What discussion questions do you have for other readers, for the authors, or for self-reflection to explore more from this chapter?

Unit Plan Organizer

Subject: Grade level:	Unit of study:
Approximate length of unit: Number of days to reteach or enrich: Dates:	Essential questions of unit:

Standards covered in this unit (CCSS ELA and essential standards for your content area):

Concepts they will learn (what students need to know):	Skills students need to be able to do:

Engaging activities, tasks, or learning experiences (projects, graphic organizers, group simulations, research, plays, presentations, and so on):

Vocabulary web of words learned during this unit (can use back of page):

Resources, materials, technology, or texts:

Engaging Lesson Plan Template

Unit, theme, or topic: _____

STANDARDS	MATERIALS, TEXTS, OR TECHNOLOGY
Daily target and assessment (Do, Know, Show): Engagement zones: _____ Length of lesson: _____	Criteria for success: ☐ Rubric ☐ Checklist ☐ Exemplar ☐ Conferencing ☐ Peer or self-evaluation ☐ Teacher observation or notes ☐ Other: _____
Agenda/tasks/activities/strategies:	Engagement and CCSS strategies: ☐ Group work ☐ Game ☐ Creativity ☐ Problem solving ☐ Critical thinking ☐ Movement or kinesthetic activity ☐ Experiment ☐ Reading ☐ Writing ☐ Speaking and listening ☐ Technology ☐ Other: _____
Differentiation ideas: Vocabulary to explore: Higher-level questions to ask:	Formative assessments used: ☐ Teacher observation ☐ Written response or drawing ☐ Verbal response ☐ Self-assessment ☐ Sentios (electronic voting machines) or other technology ☐ Door passes ☐ Quick checks (dry-erase boards and so on) ☐ Question and answer ☐ Other: _____

Door Passes

Door Pass	Door Pass
Name: _____ Date: _____	Name: _____ Date: _____
Door Pass	Door Pass
Name: _____ Date: _____	Name: _____ Date: _____

APPENDIX A

INCORPORATING DIFFERENTIATION

Differentiation can take many forms. Remember, differentiation involves responding to your students' needs in order to help them learn to their fullest potential. It is changing the regular path or plan that you might have in order to help the student achieve or surpass the standard. Here we list several ways to approach differentiating your classroom, from planning the lesson to closing the lesson. We cover how to differentiate lesson plans and preassessments; the standard, target, and criteria for success; the Cha-Cha-Chas; and the lesson closure.

Lesson Plans and Preassessments

Know your students well so you can set them up for success. Think through these pieces before writing your lesson plan:

- The learning profile (a file folder of information about your students); you'll need to know each student's—
  - Feelings about subject area
  - Reading level (decoding, comprehension, fluency, and so on)
  - Writing sample
  - Math problem-solving ability and known math facts
  - Family life
  - Multiple intelligences
  - Interests
  - Learning preferences
- Your rules, routines, and rituals in place—have students help create these
- The type of groups that will need to be formed for success with this outcome
- The content you will prime or pre-expose their brains to based on what you know about them
- The 504 and IEP strategies that must be included within this lesson
- Challenges or misconceptions that could occur within this lesson and how you might support the learner with them

- Potential challenging behaviors that need to be addressed during this lesson
- Whether you will differentiate the content, process, or product for student success

You also need to know what your students already know. Give preassessments days or weeks before teaching the concept. You can use any of the following:

- Unit or chapter summative assessment given at least two weeks before starting unit
- Quizzes that reflect a small section of learning given before a lesson
- Formative assessment from previous days' lessons
- Vocabulary word quiz (cloze activity, matching, guess the meaning, and so on)
- Paragraph writing about students' background knowledge on topic
- Quick picture drawn on topic
- Quick list of facts
- Alphabet brainstorm (list words on a particular topic and place them in categories by first letter of alphabet) and other brainstorms
- Questions and potential answers
- Cumulative data
- Clipboard observations
- Surveys or polls

The Standard, Target, and Criteria for Success

To differentiate the presentation of the *standard*, write out the essential questions that the students will answer within one specific lesson (not the whole unit—unit essential questions will be placed in the unit plan). Post these questions in your classroom.

To differentiate your *targets*, try writing them as "I Can" statements and in student-friendly language. Then explain them and post them in the classroom. Try to combine two or more "I Can" statements to make a powerful one (social studies and language arts, science and math, and so on).

Select a higher-level verb for the Do stage that shows the level of processing. For Know, list the specific content that students will be learning. Make sure it can be measured within one to three days. For Show, make sure all products show student mastery of the target. You can use any of the following:

- Graphic organizers
- Journal entries
- Technology used in products and presentations
- Tic-tac-toe grid of product choices
- Product choices that range in options for multiple intelligences, gender, culture, and race
- Analogies, diagrams, demonstrations, presentations, open-ended response, on-demand writing, portfolios
- Learning contracts

The *criteria for success* can be differentiated by changing sections of rubrics or checklists to scaffold for success.

The Cha-Cha-Chas

Here are ways the Cha-Cha-Chas—chunk, chew, check, change—can help you differentiate the content, process, and assessments, as well as adjust your approach midcourse.

Chunk

There are many ways to differentiate the content chunks. For instance, you can differentiate content by allowing students diverse points of access:

- Use various levels of texts, journals, websites, online articles, magazine articles, and so on.
- Allow students to access different websites to find content, answer questions, or complete projects. Webquests are a great way to accomplish this; visit www.webquest.org for more information about webquests.
- Vary your use of audio and video recordings.
- Take advantage of peer and adult mentors.
- Model and use research methods such as the Big 6.
- Use literature circles or guided reading groups to teach content at various levels.
- Deliver content in a variety of ways, such as explicit instruction from teacher, jigsaws with students, DVDs, the Internet, blogs, guest speakers, and so on.
- Make use of reciprocal teaching and QAR (Question-Answer Relationship—a research-based reading and questioning strategy to improve comprehension).
- Present ideas through both auditory and visual means including graphic organizers, flip charts, and other charts and models.
- Use varied manipulatives and resources.
- Build anticipation guides into your lessons.
- Use multimedia presentations.
- Use interest centers for additional exploration.
- Use student interests and events in students' lives as examples in content areas.
- Use diversity regarding race, gender, and cultures.
- Incorporate multiple intelligences and learning styles into the content.
- Introduce varied note-taking strategies matched up to student learning needs.
- Use Thinking Maps (www.thinkingmaps.com).
- Gradually release responsibility from you to the students by modeling, explaining, providing analogies and examples, and so on.

- Tier the target. Take the target and make it more challenging or complex for those who have shown you they are ready for it. Or take the target and make it less complex with scaffolding in place to help the students reach the target.

Chew

There are many ways to differentiate the process. This step relates to the verb in the target you chose—it's how the students make the content meaningful.

- Create tiered activities with the same content but different levels of difficulty.

- Vary the reflection questions. For instance, use different question stems for different students.

- Provide interest centers and centers with the standards from the unit as the focus.

- Use hands-on materials.

- Vary pacing according to each student's readiness.

- Have the class participate in literature circles, debates, and Socratic seminars.

- Provide metacognitive task choices at varying levels.

- Provide goal-setting templates to help students think through and accomplish goals.

- Incorporate cooperative learning activities into the target.

- Allow students to choose strategies for processing information, and provide a variety of ways for students to express the results of that processing. For instance, let students choose how to process the content or notes in their Interactive Notebooks.

- Allow for working alone, in partners, in triads, and in small groups.

- Use a variety of thinking verbs within the objective: *apply, analyze, synthesize, evaluate, sort, elaborate,* and so on.

- Discover and experiment.

- Incorporate student-generated prompts, word problems, and questions into the learning process.

- Provide different homework options for student success.

- Allow for varied journal responses.

- Use a variety of anchor activities for students to do when they have completed their work or the teacher is working with a small group.

- Go from both part to whole and whole to part. Some students learn better by seeing the parts first, then the wholes; while other students need to see the whole picture to understand the parts (inductive and deductive reasoning).

Check

There are many ways to differentiate the formative assessments. This step relates to how you plan to check for understanding and what you will do with the data that you observe or collect. This is done *during* the lesson several times. Combine the various types of assessments with different products to display the data to create endless differentiation possibilities (see table A.1).

Table A.1: Differentiating Formative Assessments

GENERAL TYPES OF FORMATIVE ASSESSMENTS	PRODUCTS TO DISPLAY THE TANGIBLE DATA
• Writing • Drawing • Verbal explanation • Question and answer • Answer essential questions • Solve math problems • Generate questions • Self-assessment	• Door passes • Dry-erase, gel, minichalkboards • Sentios (electronic voting machines) • Paper • Verbal or clipboard documentation • Sticky notes • Note cards • Teacher observation

Change

There are many ways to differentiate a lesson midcourse in response to preassessments, learning profiles, and formative assessments. The heart of differentiation is to evaluate the daily data from our students' work and let it drive our instruction while changing what we are doing so we can better meet the instructional needs of the students.

- Group students homogenously based on readiness levels. Pull small groups aside and quickly reteach *or* enrich with challenging activities; plan the groups ahead of time to tier the activities.

- Group students homogeneously based on what you see in their learning profiles so they help each other grow in their strong areas. Use data about their multiple intelligences, the way they like to process, interests they have, and so on.

- Group students heterogeneously so there is a mix of ideas, readiness levels, interests, strengths, multiple intelligences, and so on.

- Spiral the target back in later in the lesson.

- Add the target to the warm-up the next day.

- Include the target in a door pass.

- Reteach *differently* from original teaching—use small groups, half the class, or whole groups excluding the few who mastered it.

- Reteach in the strongest or most dominant multiple intelligence or learning style of the struggling student.

- Change and adjust the flexible groups.

- Use an anchor activity if working with small groups so others stay on task.

- Create enriching activities, or compact the curriculum for those who showed mastery.

- Create a tiered lesson for the next day.

- Assign peer tutors.

- Continue to review the concept throughout the week as often as needed.

- Prepare games to review content and then recheck for mastery.

- Plan a quiz (which also rechecks mastery) so that students know they are held accountable on that particular day. Be sure to tell them what and how to study.

Following are some ideas to make the target more challenging:

- Give students more choices.

- Make the assignment more broad or abstract, and have them deal with the details.

- Use more challenging verbs.

- Have students generate questions about the learning.

- For writing assignments, expectations could be more complex sentences, more sophisticated vocabulary, several turning points and figurative language, and so on.

Following are some ideas to decrease the complexity of the target for struggling students:

- Create a template for students to fill in faster so they can think about the content more.

- Reteach with a different strategy.

- Use VAK (visual, auditory, and kinesthetic) strategies for every lesson.

- Assign study buddies.

- Color code information as much as possible—use highlighters for words and thoughts during reading, editing marks, mindmapping, and so on.

- Give students question stems and sentence starters to help them get started with conversations and writing.

- Allow them to verbalize and summarize what they learned after small chunks of acquiring information.

Lesson Closure

Closures check to see if students reached the target. They should only take about three to four minutes, and every student must engage in them. The product can be written or verbal.

Some examples of closure stems include:

- To summarize, I learned _____.

- The most important things to understand are _____.

- This concept is related to these other concepts because _____.

- Remember to _____ when solving _____ math problem.

- The main idea of _____ is _____.

- The word _____ means _____.

- I'm beginning to wonder _____ now that I have learned _____.

- Some examples of _____ are _____.

- In my opinion, _____.

- I believe _____ is beneficial/harmful/dangerous because _____.

- I think _____ is necessary/unimportant because _____.

- I feel _____ is important because _____.

- I used to feel/believe _____, but now I feel/believe _____ because _____.

- Here is a possible way to solve the following problem: _____.

- Some details that I learned today are _____.

- I have the following questions that should help me understand _____ better.

- I made a personal connection with _____ because _____.

Some examples of closure activities include:

- Choose one event from your reading to elaborate on.

- Illustrate what you learned or visualized while reading.

- Solve this problem.

- Give an example of how one event from the reading supports our theme.

Differentiating each strategy is the key to making sure every student succeeds. Some strategies require very specific ways to differentiate, while others could use a variety of techniques from this list. Remember, know your students, know your curriculum, and tailor the strategies so all students can reach your daily targets.

MATCHING THE ENGAGEMENT STRATEGIES WITH ANCHOR STANDARDS

The strategies listed here have the potential to meet the Common Core Reading and Writing anchor standards marked with an *x*, depending on how the teacher uses the strategy. We created these tables to help you see how the strategies could help students meet certain Common Core Reading and Writing anchor standards. If there is a particular anchor standard that stumps you, find it and try one of the suggested strategies in your lessons.

Reading Strand

Following are the Common Core anchor standards for Reading (NGA & CCSSO, 2010, p. 10).

- **CCRA.R.1:** Read closely to determine what the text says explicitly and to make logical inferences from it; cite specific textual evidence when writing or speaking to support conclusions drawn from the text.

- **CCRA.R.2:** Determine central ideas or themes of a text and analyze their development; summarize the key supporting details and ideas.

- **CCRA.R.3:** Analyze how and why individuals, events, or ideas develop and interact over the course of a text.

- **CCRA.R.4:** Interpret words and phrases as they are used in a text, including determining technical, connotative, and figurative meanings, and analyze how specific word choices shape meaning or tone.

- **CCRA.R.5:** Analyze the structure of texts, including how specific sentences, paragraphs, and larger portions of the text (e.g., a section, chapter, scene, or stanza) relate to each other and the whole.

- **CCRA.R.6:** Assess how point of view or purpose shapes the content and style of a text.

- **CCRA.R.7:** Integrate and evaluate content presented in diverse media and formats, including visually and quantitatively, as well as in words.*

- **CCRA.R.8:** Delineate and evaluate the argument and specific claims in a text, including the validity of the reasoning as well as the relevance and sufficiency of the evidence.

- **CCRA.R.9:** Analyze how two or more texts address similar themes or topics in order to build knowledge or to compare the approaches the authors take.

- **CCRA.R.10:** Read and comprehend complex literary and informational texts independently and proficiently.

* Please see "Research to Build and Present Knowledge" in Writing and "Comprehension and Collaboration" in Speaking and Listening for additional standards relevant to gathering, assessing, and applying information from print and digital sources.

Table B.1: Matching Zone 1 Engagement Strategies With the Common Core Reading Anchor Standards

	1	2	3	4	5	6	7	8	9	10
1. Pre-Exposure and Priming	X	X	X	X	X	X	X	X	X	X
2. *The Important Book*	X	X						X	X	X
3. Historical Event Web	X		X							X
4. Kinesthetic Vocabulary				X						
5. Super Sleuth	X	X	X	X	X	X	X	X	X	X
6. Activating Prior Knowledge Dice	X	X	X	X	X	X	X	X	X	X
7. List-Sort-Label-Write				X						
8. Carousel Brainstorm	X	X	X	X	X	X	X	X	X	X
9. Skimming and Scanning	X				X					X
10. Reporter Goes Big Time	X						X		X	X

Table B.2: Matching Zone 2 Engagement Strategies With the Common Core Reading Anchor Standards

	1	2	3	4	5	6	7	8	9	10
11. The Big 6 Research Process	X	X						X	X	X
12. Produce, Improve, Prioritize										
13. Brainstorming Bonanza	X	X		X			X			X
14. Finding Credible and Accurate Resources	X					X			X	X
15. Speak What You Know	Speaking and Listening anchor standards									
16. Quad Cards	X	X		X						X
17. Reflective Conversations	X	X		X						X
18. H Diagram				X					X	
19. Stump the Chump	X			X						X

Table B.3: Matching Zone 3 Engagement Strategies With the Common Core Reading Anchor Standards

	1	2	3	4	5	6	7	8	9	10
20. Close Reading Steps	X	X	X	X	X	X	X	X	X	X
21. Close Reading Marks	X	X	X	X	X	X	X	X	X	X
22. Three Short Summaries for Nonfiction		X								
23. Fix-It Activities	X	X	X	X	X	X	X	X	X	X
24. Reciprocal Teaching With Nonfiction	X	X	X	X	X	X	X	X	X	X
25. Mindmapping for Solutions	X	X		X	X			X	X	X
26. Stop-n-Think	X	X	X	X	X	X	X	X	X	X
27. Interactive Notebook	X	X	X	X	X	X	X	X	X	X
28. Walking in the Shoes of Another	X	X				X	X	X	X	X
29. Six Thinking Hats	X	X	X	X	X	X	X	X	X	X
30. Socratic Seminars	X									X

Writing Strand

Following are the Common Core anchor standards for Writing (NGA & CCSSO, 2010, p. 18).

- **CCRA.W.1:** Write arguments to support claims in an analysis of substantive topics or texts using valid reasoning and relevant and sufficient evidence.
- **CCRA.W.2:** Write informative/explanatory texts to examine and convey complex ideas and information clearly and accurately through the effective selection, organization, and analysis of content.
- **CCRA.W.3:** Write narratives to develop real or imagined experiences or events using effective technique, well-chosen details and well-structured event sequences.
- **CCRA.W.4:** Produce clear and coherent writing in which the development, organization, and style are appropriate to task, purpose, and audience.
- **CCRA.W.5:** Develop and strengthen writing as needed by planning, revising, editing, rewriting, or trying a new approach.
- **CCRA.W.6:** Use technology, including the Internet, to produce and publish writing and to interact and collaborate with others.
- **CCRA.W.7:** Conduct short as well as more sustained research projects based on focused questions, demonstrating understanding of the subject under investigation.
- **CCRA.W.8:** Gather relevant information from multiple print and digital sources, assess the credibility and accuracy of each source, and integrate the information while avoiding plagiarism.
- **CCRA.W.9:** Draw evidence from literary or informational texts to support analysis, reflection, and research.
- **CCRA.W.10:** Write routinely over extended time frames (time for research, reflection, and revision) and shorter time frames (a single sitting or a day or two) for a range of tasks, purposes, and audiences.

Table B.4: Matching Zone 1 Engagement Strategies With the Common Core Writing Anchor Standards

	1	2	3	4	5	6	7	8	9	10
1. Pre-Exposure and Priming	X	X	X	X	X	X	X	X	X	X
2. *The Important Book*	X					X			X	
3. Historical Event Web		X	X	X	X		X		X	
4. Kinesthetic Vocabulary										
5. Super Sleuth	X	X	X	X	X	X	X	X	X	X
6. Activating Prior Knowledge Dice	X	X	X	X	X	X	X	X	X	X
7. List-Sort-Label-Write		X		X	X	X	X		X	X
8. Carousel Brainstorm	X	X	X	X	X	X	X	X	X	X
9. Skimming and Scanning										X
10. Reporter Goes Big Time							X			X

Table B.5: Matching Zone 2 Engagement Strategies With the Common Core Writing Anchor Standards

	1	2	3	4	5	6	7	8	9	10
11. The Big 6 Research Process	X	X		X	X	X	X	X	X	X
12. Produce, Improve, Prioritize							X			
13. Brainstorming Bonanza						X	X	X	X	
14. Finding Credible and Accurate Resources								X	X	
15. Speak What You Know	Speaking and Listening anchor standards									
16. Quad Cards										X
17. Reflective Conversations	Speaking and Listening anchor standards									
18. H Diagram		X		X	X					X
19. Stump the Chump										

Table B.6: Matching Zone 3 Engagement Strategies With the Common Core Writing Anchor Standards

	1	2	3	4	5	6	7	8	9	10
20. Close Reading Steps	X	X	X	X	X	X	X	X	X	X
21. Close Reading Marks	X	X	X	X	X	X	X	X	X	X
22. Three Short Summaries for Nonfiction									X	X
23. Fix-It Activities										X
24. Reciprocal Teaching With Nonfiction										X
25. Mindmapping for Solutions	X	X	X	X	X	X	X	X	X	X
26. Stop-n-Think	X	X	X	X	X	X	X	X	X	X
27. Interactive Notebook	X	X	X	X	X	X	X	X	X	X
28. Walking in the Shoes of Another	X	X							X	X
29. Six Thinking Hats	X	X	X	X	X	X	X	X	X	X
30. Socratic Seminars	X	X	X	X	X	X	X	X	X	X

REFERENCES AND RESOURCES

ACT. (2006). *Reading between the lines: What the ACT reveals about college readiness in reading.* Iowa City, IA: Author. Accessed at www.act.org/research/policymakers/pdf/reading_summary.pdf on September 6, 2013.

ACT. (2009). *The condition of college readiness 2009.* Iowa City, IA: Author.

Adams, M. J. (2009). The challenge of advanced texts: The interdependence of reading and learning. In E. H. Hiebert (Ed.), *Reading more, reading better: Are American students reading enough of the right stuff?* (pp. 163–189). New York: Guilford Press.

Allen, L. G., & Nickelsen, L. (2008). *Making words their own: Building foundations for powerful vocabularies.* Peterborough, NH: Crystal Springs Books.

Anderson, L., & Krathwohl, D. (Eds.). (2001). *A taxonomy for learning, teaching, and assessing: A revision of Bloom's taxonomy of educational objectives.* New York: Longman.

Association for Supervision and Curriculum Development. (2003). What professional development structures best affect classroom instruction? *Translating Education Research Into Action, 1*(15), 1–4.

Aud, S., Hussar, W., Kena, G., Bianco, K., Frohlich, L., Kemp, J., et al. (2011). *The condition of education 2011.* Washington, DC: National Center for Education Statistics.

Baker, S., & Smith, S. (1999). Starting off on the right foot: The influence of four principles of professional development in improving literacy instruction in two kindergarten programs. *Learning Disabilities Research and Practice, 14*(4), 239–253.

Beck, I., McKeown, M., & Kucan, L. (2002). *Bringing words to life: Robust vocabulary instruction.* New York: Guilford Press.

Beers, K., & Probst, R. E. (2013). *Notice and note: Strategies for close reading.* Portsmouth, NH: Heinemann.

Birman, B. F., Desimone, L., Garet, M. S., & Porter, A. C. (2000). Designing professional development that works. *Educational Leadership, 57*(8), 28–33.

Black, P., & Wiliam, D. (1998a). Assessment and classroom learning. *Assessment in Education: Principles, Policy, and Practice, 5*(1), 7–73.

Black, P., & Wiliam, D. (1998b). Inside the black box: Raising standards through classroom assessment. *Phi Delta Kappan, 80*(2), 139–149.

Brown, M. W. (1949). *The important book.* New York: HarperCollins.

Calkins, L., Ehrenworth, M., & Lehman, C. (2012). *Pathways to the Common Core: Accelerating achievement.* Portsmouth, NH: Heinemann.

Cave, B. (1997). Very long-lasting priming in picture naming. *Psychological Science, 8*(4), 322–325.

Chouinard, M. M. (2007). Children's questions: A mechanism for cognitive development. *Monographs of the Society for Research in Child Development, 72*(1), i, v, vii–ix, 1–129.

Cohen, D. K., & Hill, H. C. (2001). *Learning policy: When state education reform works.* New Haven, CT: Yale University Press.

Conley, D. T. (2010). *College and career ready: Helping all students succeed beyond high school.* San Francisco: Jossey-Bass.

Covington, M. V. (1992). *Making the grade: A self-worth perspective on motivation and school reform.* New York: Cambridge University Press.

Covington, M. V. (1999). Caring about learning: The nature and nurturing of subject-matter appreciation. *Educational Psychologist, 34*(2), 127–136.

Darling-Hammond, L., Barron, B., Pearson, D., Schoenfeld, A., Stage, E., Zimmerman, T., et al. (2008). *Powerful learning: What we know about teaching for understanding.* San Francisco: Jossey-Bass.

de Bono, E. (1999). *Six thinking hats.* New York: Little, Brown.

Deci, E. L., Koestner, R., & Ryan, R. M. (1999). A meta-analytic review of experiments examining the effects of extrinsic rewards on intrinsic motivation. *Psychological Bulletin, 125*(6), 627–668.

Dimberg, U., & Thunberg, M. (1998). Rapid facial reactions to different emotionally relevant stimuli. *Scandinavian Journal of Psychology, 39*, 39–45.

Duhigg, C. (2012). *The power of habit: Why we do what we do in life and business.* New York: Random House.

Durlak, J. A., Weissberg, R. P., Dymnicki, A. B., Taylor, R. D., & Schellinger, K. B. (2011). The impact of enhancing students' social and emotional learning: A meta-analysis of school-based universal interventions. *Child Development, 82*(1), 405–432.

Dutro, E., Fisk, M. C., Koch, R., Roop, L. J., & Wixson, K. (2002). When state policies meet local district contexts: Standards-based professional development as a means to individual agency and collective ownership. *Teachers College Record, 104*, 787–811.

Dweck, C. (2006). *Mindset: The new psychology of success.* New York: Ballantine.

Eisenberg, M. B., & Berkowitz, R. E. (1999). *Teaching information & technology skills: The big 6 in elementary schools.* Worthington, OH: Linworth Books.

Ericsson, K. A., Krampe, R. T., & Tesch-Romer, C. (1993). The role of deliberate practice in the acquisition of expert performance. *Psychological Review, 100*, 363–406.

Fisher, D. (2013). *What is close reading?* Accessed at www.mhecommoncoretoolboxfl.com/what-is-close -reading.html on May 31, 2013.

Fisher, D., Frey, N., & Lapp, D. (2012). *Text complexity: Raising the rigor in reading.* Newark, DE: International Reading Association.

Fountas, I. C., & Pinnell, G. S. (2001). *Guiding readers and writers: Teaching comprehension, genre, and content literacy.* Portsmouth, NH: Heinemann.

Fredericks, J., Blumenfeld, P., & Paris, A. (2004). School engagement: Potential of the concept, and state of the evidence. *Review of Educational Research*, *74*(1), 59–109.

Fuchs, L. S., & Fuchs, D. (1986). Effects of systematic formative evaluation: A meta-analysis. *Exceptional Children*, *53*(3), 199–208.

Gallagher, K. (2012). *Write like this: Teaching real-world writing through modeling and mentor texts*. Portland, ME: Stenhouse.

Graves, M., & Graves, B. (1994). *Scaffolding reading experiences: Designs for student success*. Norwood, MA: Christopher-Gordon.

Hafen, C. A., Allen, J. P., Mikami, A. Y., Gregory, A., Hamre, B., & Pianta, R. C. (2012). The pivotal role of adolescent autonomy in secondary school classrooms. *Journal of Youth and Adolescence*, *41*(3), 245–255.

Hattie, J. (2009). *Visible learning: A synthesis of over 800 meta-analyses relating to achievement*. New York: Routledge.

Hattie, J. (2012). *Visible learning for teachers: Maximizing impact on learning*. New York: Routledge.

Jackson, R. R. (2011). *How to plan rigorous instruction: Mastering the principles of great teaching*. Alexandria, VA: Association for Supervision and Curriculum Development.

Jago, C. (2011). *With rigor for all: Meeting Common Core standards for reading literature* (2nd ed.). Portsmouth, NH: Heinemann.

Jensen, E., & Nickelsen, L. (2008). *Deeper learning: 7 powerful strategies for in-depth and longer-lasting learning*. Thousand Oaks, CA: Corwin Press.

Kendall, J. (2011). *Understanding the Common Core State Standards*. Alexandria, VA: Association for Supervision and Curriculum Development.

Kirby, E., Muroy, S. E., Sun, W. G., Covarrubias, D., Leong, M. J., Barchas, L. A., et al. (2013, April 16). Acute stress enhances adult rat hippocampal neurogenesis and activation of newborn neurons via secreted astrocytic FGF2. *eLife*. Accessed at http://elife.elifesciences.org/content/2/e00362 on September 5, 2013.

Klamath Falls City Schools. (n.d.). *All about writing essential questions*. Klamath Falls, OR: Author. Accessed at www.kfalls.k12.or.us/kuhs/Seniors/Senior%20project/Writing%20Essential%20Questions.pdf on October 14, 2013.

Klem, A. M., & Connell, J. P. (2004). Relationships matter: Linking teacher support to student engagement and achievement. *Journal of School Health*, *74*(7), 262–273.

Laflamme, J. G. (1997). The effect of the multiple exposure vocabulary method and the target reading strategy on test scores. *Journal of Adolescent and Adult Literacy*, *40*(5), 372–381.

Lindström, B. R., & Bohlin, G. (2012). Threat-relevance impairs executive functions: Negative impact on working memory and response inhibition. *Emotion*, *12*(2), 384–393.

Loomis, J. M., Klatzky, R. L., McHugh, B., & Giudice, N. A. (2012). Spatial working memory for locations specified by vision and audition: Testing the amodality hypothesis. *Attention, Perception, & Psychophysics*, *74*(6), 1260–1267.

Marks, H. M. (2000). Student engagement in instructional activity: Patterns in the elementary, middle, and high school years. *American Educational Research Journal*, *37*(1), 153–184.

Martin, A. (2001). Functional neuroimaging of semantic memory. In R. Cabeza & A. Ingstone (Eds.), *Handbook of functional neuroimaging of cognition* (pp. 153–186). Cambridge: Massachusetts Institute of Technology Press.

Martin, A., & van Turennout, M. (2002). Searching for the neural correlates of object priming. In D. L. Schacter & L. R. Squire (Eds.), *Neuropsychology of memory* (3rd ed., pp. 239–247). New York: Guildford Press.

Marzano, R. J., & Pickering, D. J. (2011). *The highly engaged classroom*. Bloomington, IN: Marzano Research Laboratory.

Marzano, R. J., Pickering, D. J., & Pollock, J. E. (2001). *Classroom instruction that works: Research-based strategies for increasing student achievement*. Alexandria, VA: Association for Supervision and Curriculum Development.

Marzano, R. J., Yanoski, D. C., Hoegh, J. K., & Simms, J. A. (2013). *Using Common Core standards to enhance classroom instruction and assessment*. Bloomington, IN: Marzano Research Laboratory.

Mayer, J. D., Caruso, D. R., & Salovey, P. (2000). Emotional intelligence meets traditional standards for an intelligence. *Intelligence, 27*(4), 267–298. Accessed at www.unh.edu/emotional_intelligence/EIAssets/EmotionalIntelligenceProper/EI1999MayerCarusoSaloveyIntelligence.pdf on September 6, 2013.

Mehta, R., & Zhu, R. J. (2009). Blue or red? Exploring the effect of color on cognitive task performances. *Science, 323*(5918), 1226–1229.

McGettigan, C., Warren, J. E., Eisner, F., Marshall, C. R., Shanmugalingam, P., & Scott, S. K. (2011). Neural correlates of sublexical processing in phonological working memory. *Journal of Cognitive Neuroscience, 23*(4), 961–977.

McTighe, J., & Wiggins, G. (2013). *Essential questions: Opening doors to student understanding*. Alexandria, VA: Association for Supervision and Curriculum Development.

National Assessment Governing Board. (2008). *Reading framework for the 2009 National Assessment of Educational Progress*. Washington, DC: U.S. Government Printing Office.

National Assessment Governing Board. (2010). *Writing framework for the 2011 National Assessment of Educational Progress*. Iowa City, IA: ACT. Accessed at www.nagb.org/content/nagb/assets/documents/publications/frameworks/writing-2011.pdf on October 14, 2013.

National Center for School Engagement. (2006). *Quantifying school engagement: Research report*. Denver: Colorado Foundation for Families and Children.

National Geographic Society. (2009). *Garden helpers*. Accessed at http://ngexplorer.cengage.com/ngyoungexplorer/0909/readstory.html on July 2, 2013.

National Governors Association Center for Best Practices & Council of Chief State School Officers. (n.d.a). *Common Core State Standards for English language arts & literacy in history/social studies, science, and technical subjects: Appendix B—Text exemplars and sample performance tasks*. Washington, DC: Authors. Accessed at www.corestandards.org/assets/Appendix_B.pdf on October 15, 2013.

National Governors Association Center for Best Practices & Council of Chief State School Officers. (n.d.b). *Common Core State Standards for English language arts & literacy in history/social studies, science, and technical subjects: Appendix C—Samples of student writing*. Washington, DC: Authors. Accessed at www.corestandards.org/assets/Appendix_C.pdf on October 15, 2013.

National Governors Association Center for Best Practices & Council of Chief State School Officers. (2010). *Common Core State Standards for English language arts and literacy in history/social studies, science, & technical subjects*. Washington, DC: Authors.

National Governors Association Center for Best Practices & Council of Chief State School Officers. (2012a). *Myths vs. facts*. Accessed at www.corestandards.org/resources/myths-vs-facts on June 4, 2013.

National Governors Association Center for Best Practices & Council of Chief State School Officers. (2012b). *English language arts standards: Introduction—Key design consideration*. Accessed at www.core standards.org/ELA-Literacy/introduction/key-design-consideration on September 6, 2013.

National Governors Association Center for Best Practices & Council of Chief State School Officers. (2012c). *Mission statement*. Accessed at www.corestandards.org on July 1, 2013.

National Reading Panel. (2002). *Teaching children to read*. Jessup, MD: National Institute for Literacy at ED Publishing.

Nickelsen, L. (2004). *Comprehension mini-lessons: Main idea and summarizing*. New York: Scholastic Teaching Resources.

No Child Left Behind (NCLB) Act of 2001, Pub. L. No. 107-110, § 115, Stat. 1425 (2002).

Organisation for Economic Co-operation and Development. (2010). *PISA 2009 results: What students know and can do—Student performance in reading, mathematics and science* (Vol. 1). Paris: Author. Accessed at http://dx.doi.org/10.1787/9789264091450-en on September 10, 2013.

Public Schools Accountability Act of 1999, Cal. Educ. Code §§52050-52050.5 (1999).

Rasinski, T. (2010). *Effective teaching of reading: From phonics to fluency*. Newark, NJ: International Reading Association.

Reeves, D. (2003). *High performance in high poverty schools: 90/90/90 and beyond*. Accessed at www.nsbsd .org/Page/705 on July 2, 2013.

Rothstein, D., & Santana, L. (2011). *Make just one change: Teach students to ask their own questions*. Cambridge, MA: Harvard Education Press.

Rutman, A. M., Clapp, W. C., Chadick, J. Z., & Gazzaley, A. (2010). Early top-down control of visual processing predicts working memory performance. *Journal of Cognitive Neuroscience, 22*(6), 1224–1234.

Sadler, D. R. (1989). Formative assessment and the design of instructional systems. *Instructional Science, 18*, 119–144.

Sanders, W. L., & Rivers, J. C. (1996). *Cumulative and residual effects of teachers on future students' academic achievement*. Knoxville: University of Tennessee Value-Added Research and Assessment Center. Accessed at www.mccsc.edu/~curriculum/cumulative%20and%20residual%20effects%20of%20 teachers.pdf on December 12, 2012.

Schmoker, M., & Marzano, R. J. (1999). Using standards and assessments: Realizing the promise of standards-based education. *Educational Leadership, 56*(6), 17–21.

Shanahan, T. (2012). The Common Core ate my baby and other urban legends. *Educational Leadership, 70*(4), 11–16. Accessed at www.ascd.org/publications/educational-leadership/dec12/vol70/num04 /The-Common-Core-Ate-My-Baby-and-Other-Urban-Legends.aspx on September 9, 2013.

Silver, H., Dewing, T, & Perini, M. (2012). *The core six: Essential strategies for achieving excellence with the Common Core*. Alexandria, VA: Association for Supervision and Curriculum Development.

Skinner, E. A., Kindermann, T. A., Connell, J. P., & Wellborn, J. G. (2009). Engagement as an organizational construct in the dynamics of motivational development. In K. R. Wentzel & A. Wigfield (Eds.), *Handbook of motivation at school* (pp. 223–245). New York: Routledge.

Sloan, W. (2010). *Coming to terms with Common Core Standards*. Accessed at www.ascd.org/publications /newsletters/policy-priorities/vol16/issue4/full/Coming-to-Terms-with-Common-Core-Standards.aspx on September 3, 2013.

Stiggins, R., & Chappuis. J. (2005). Using student-involved classroom assessment to close achievement gaps. *Theory Into Practice*, *44*(1), 11–18.

Thaler, R., & Sunstein, C. (2008). *Nudge: Improving decisions about health, wealth, and happiness*. New Haven, CT: Yale University Press.

ThinkCERCA. (2013). *About us*. Accessed at http://thinkcerca.com on September 11, 2013.

Tovani, C. (2011). *So what do they really know? Assessment that informs teaching and learning*. Markham, Ontario, Canada: Pembroke.

van Turennout, M., Bielamowicz, L., & Martin, A. (2003). Modulation of neural activity during object naming: Effects of time and practice. *Cerebral Cortex*, *13*(4), 381–391.

Vedhara, K., Hyde, J., Gilchrist, I. D., Tytherleigh, M., & Plummer, S. (2000). Acute stress, memory, attention and cortisol. *Psychoneuroendocrinology*, *6*, 535–549.

Wiggins, G., & McTighe, J. (2005). *Understanding by design* (2nd ed.). Alexandria, VA: Association for Supervision and Curriculum Development.

Wiliam, D. (2007). Keeping learning on track: Formative assessment and the regulation of learning. In F. K. Lester, Jr. (Ed.), *Second handbook of mathematics teaching & learning* (pp. 1053–1098). Greenwich, CT: Information Age.

Wormeli, R. (2006). *Fair isn't always equal: Assessing and grading in the differentiated classroom*. Portland, ME: Stenhouse.

Yazzie-Mintz, E. (2010). *Charting the path from engagement to achievement: A report on the 2009 high school survey of student engagement*. Bloomington, IN: Center for Evaluation & Education Policy.

Zee, M., Koomen, H. M., & Van der Veen, I. (2013). Student-teacher relationship quality and academic adjustment in upper elementary school: The role of student personality. *Journal of School Psychology*, *51*(4), 517–533.

Zull, J. E. (2002). *The art of changing the brain: Enriching the practice of teaching by exploring the biology of learning*. Sterling, VA: Stylus.

INDEX

How to Teach Thinking Skills Within the Common Core
James A. Bellanca, Robin J. Fogarty, and Brian M. Pete
Empower your students to thrive across the curriculum. Packed with examples and tools, this practical guide prepares teachers across all grade levels and content areas to teach the most critical cognitive skills from the Common Core State Standards.
BKF576

40 Reading Intervention Strategies for K–6 Students
Elaine K. McEwan-Adkins
This well-rounded collection of reading intervention strategies, teacher-friendly lesson plans, and adaptable miniroutines will support and inform your RTI efforts. Many of the strategies motivate all students as well as scaffold struggling readers. Increase effectiveness by using the interventions across grade-level teams or schoolwide.
BKF270

20 Literacy Strategies to Meet the Common Core
Elaine K. McEwan-Adkins and Allyson J. Burnett
With the advent of the Common Core State Standards, some secondary teachers are scrambling for what to do and how to do it. This book provides twenty research-based strategies designed to help students meet those standards and become expert readers.
BKF588

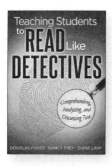

Teaching Students to Read Like Detectives
Douglas Fisher, Nancy Frey, and Diane Lapp
Prompt students to become the sophisticated readers, writers, and thinkers they need to be to achieve higher learning. Explore the important relationship between text, learner, and learning, and gain an array of methods to establish critical literacy in a discussion-based and reflective classroom.
BKF499

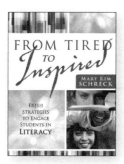

From Tired to Inspired
Mary Kim Schreck
In this Common Core State Standards–aligned book, educators will discover research-based tips and strategies to improve literacy from upper elementary to secondary school classrooms. Topics include teaching close reading and writing, engaging students, making literacy instruction meaningful, and more.
BKF594

Solution Tree | Press a division of
Solution Tree

Visit solution-tree.com or call 800.733.6786 to order.

Wait! Your professional development journey doesn't have to end with the last pages of this book.

We realize improving student learning doesn't happen overnight. And your school or district shouldn't be left to puzzle out all the details of this process alone.

No matter where you are on the journey, we're committed to helping you get to the next stage.

Take advantage of everything from **custom workshops** to **keynote presentations** and **interactive web and video conferencing**. We can even help you develop an action plan tailored to fit your specific needs.

Let's get the conversation started.

Call 888.763.9045 today.

 solution-tree.com